100 Sermon Outlines
For Personal and Group Bible Studies
To Preaching and Teaching God's Word

Joseph Jeremiah

WESTBOW
PRESS®
A DIVISION OF THOMAS NELSON
& ZONDERVAN

WestBow Press books may be ordered through booksellers or by contacting:

WestBow Press
A Division of Thomas Nelson & Zondervan
1663 Liberty Drive
Bloomington, IN 47403
www.westbowpress.com
1 (866) 928-1240

Scripture taken from the King James Version of the Bible.

ISBN: 978-1-9736-8450-3 (sc)
ISBN: 978-1-9736-8449-7 (e)

Print information available on the last page.

WestBow Press rev. date: 01/24/2020

Contents

Introduction

This book is for all readers and to assist those who preach and teach the word of God, especially those who are secularly employed but teach on Sundays and for pastors who have very busy schedules.

Foreword

As believers, our highest privilege and perhaps greatest responsibility is to faithfully share with others what the Holy Spirit has taught our own hearts from God's Word. It was Charles E Fuller, preacher of the Gospel on the *Old Fashioned Revival Hour* for thirty years, who said, "To know the Word of God, to live the Word of God, to preach the Word, to teach the Word, is the sum total of all wisdom, the heart of all Christian service".

We may not lack in desire to teach or preach the Word of God, but we may need help in learning how to develop a clear presentation of a passage or subject. Soon after I was saved at age twelve, I was asked to deliver the message from the Word of God in a morning service at a small gathering of believers, I certainly had the desire, but I seriously lacked understanding of how to prepare my chosen passage for presentation. They were some of the most embarrassing moments of my life. I say "moments" because that is about how long my message lasted!

Unfortunately, it took years before I ever attempted to share from the Word again. The blessing that resulted from that embarrassment was that I learned the value of outlining. An outline simply helps the teacher or preacher clearly present the truth of the Word of God to his or her listeners and lead them to an application of that truth to their own lives.

It has been my privilege to come to know Joseph Jeremiah over the past number of years at Hiawassa Bible Chapel in Orlando, Florida, where we both attend. As I have had opportunity to spend time with Joe, what has stood out to me is his love for our Lord Jesus Christ, his devotion to the

Word of God, and his eagerness to assist other believers in sharing the truth of the Word of God. Along with his desire to help others share the Word., *for personal and group bible study to preaching and teaching God's word.*

God has well prepared Joe for writing this book. Soon after Joe trusted in Jesus Christ at age twenty-one, he began to be active in teaching Sunday Schools and preaching on the island of Grenada, West Indies, where he was born. Over the years, the Lord has opened up opportunities for Joe to carry on a teaching and preaching ministry that has taken him to many Caribbean islands, the US Virgin Islands, thirty-one out of the fifty states in the United States, Canada, Nigeria, Africa, Guyana, South America, as well as England and Scotland.

Joseph Jeremiah has provided the reader with 100 outlines of Scriptures passages and topics that the student of the Word can either develop or modify to enable them to fulfil their desire to teach or preach the Word of God. Within the outlines, Joseph has included insightful questions and applications, such as: "Do we fully know the condition of our churches today? Do we make inquiry so that we can know how to pray?" Also, "We should be faithful to God with whatever we have and in the best way we can. We all do not have the same strength, talents, and abilities, but God will use us as we yield and make ourselves available to Him." Whether you are beginning a ministry of teaching and preaching or have been serving the church in that capacity for many years, Joseph Jeremiah's latest book offering 100 sermon outlines will be a very useful resource for you.

Chet Plimpton
Retired missionary teacher and leader and author of *A Word in Season: Encouragement for Those Who Are Weary*

A Note from the Author

Dear Friends and Fellow Believers:

I count this a high privilege from a sovereign God, that by His sovereign grace he gave me this opportunity to share with you what he laid on my heart as I seek to fulfil my role in his great commission.

I would like you to know that as I gleaned from his word, and as he allowed me to preach and teach his word for many, many years, I felt constrained to share the same with you for two reasons. First, if you do not have the assurance that one day Christ will come and you will be caught up to meet Him in the air to be with Him in heaven, this book might be of some help in giving you that assurance. Second, if you do have that assurance and are making it known to many by witnessing, preaching, and teaching, but sometimes you are busy and rushing to prepare your messages, I hope the outlines may be of help to you.

You may not break down a passage the same way as I do for you have the liberty to prepare your own outlines, but the outlines in this book may give you an option, especially when time is limited for the preparation of your messages and review of commentaries. Therefore I humbly present this book of 100 Sermon Outlines for personal and group bible studies to preaching and teaching God's word through the various outlets for your consideration.

Joseph Jeremiah

CHAPTER 1

1 – A New Beginning—Exodus 12:1–13

*T*he Children of Israel were in Egypt experiencing great difficulties under the hand of hard Taskmasters or managers, when no one was capable to deliver them, they went to the right source, the Lord God, the Lord said "I have seen the affliction of my people, I have heard their cry, I know their sorrows, I will come down to deliver them." (Exodus 3:7–8)

1. The first month of the year; there was no such month like it before.
2. Speak unto all the people; none was exempt from the good news.
3. In the tenth day of the month they shall take every man a lamb. If the household be too small, they shall share with the next-door neighbor and (a) the whole lamb must be received, (b) adjustment must be to the lamb, not the lamb to the people, and (c) the lamb must be without blemish or spot. Ref: Heb. 9:14.
4. It is the Lord's Passover—redemption by blood.
5. When I see the blood, I will pass over you. The judgment shall not be upon you when I smite the land of Egypt. He did not say when I see the bread or when I see the bitter herbs but when I see the blood. Their salvation was only by the application of the blood on the doorpost.

Different people may have different spiritual applications to this, but may I suggest one application that I see?

First we see man being enslaved in sin as a result of Adam's transgression (Rom. 5:12). We see a day to be remembered when Christ came into the world to save sinners (Matt. 2:1; 1 Tim. 1:15). We see a message to all of us (John 3:16). We see a method to be followed: Repent and be baptized every one of you in the name of Jesus Christ for the remission of sins, and ye shall the gift of the Holy Ghost. We see the meaning of the instruction (John 5:24). We see there will be a moment of inspection when Jesus comes again (1 Thess. 4:13–18; Rev. 20:11–24). Therefore, there must be the application of the blood of Christ before we leave this earth. The name H O L Y B I B L E is interpreted as:

He
Only
Loves
You;
Best
Information
Before
Leaving
Earth.

Notes:

2 – A New Experience by Obedience—John 9:1–38

*I*n John 9:1–3 we read, "And as Jesus passed by He saw a man which was blind from his birth. His disciples asked him saying Master, who did sin this man or his parents that he was born blind; Jesus said neither, but that the works of God should be made manifest in him." Jesus then spat on the ground, made clay of the spittle, anointed the eyes of the blind man, and said; "Go wash in the pool of Siloam"; He went his way, washed, and came seeing.

From this to the end of verse 38, we see:

1. According to application with respect to our relationship with God, we see that as a result of sin we were, and some are still, spiritually blind. By going to the cross, Christ has done everything for us so that we can see (Matt. 27:50–51; 1 Cor. 15:3). The songwriter said, "Christ Jesus has done all things well."

2. The command to go wash in the pool of Siloam was direct and simple. Upon completion of the work for our redemption, Christ commanded all men everywhere to repent (Acts 17:30).

3. The man went his way, washed, and came seeing. In Acts 6:7 we read that many of the priests were obedient to the faith. As we are obedient to the command to repent, we will not be in darkness.

4. When the man received his sight, he was glad, enjoying his new life because of an obedient heart. As we are obedient to Christ, we have a satisfied mind (Romans 5:1;

5. The man testified as to what happened to him: "A man who is called Jesus made clay of his spittle, anointed my eyes, and said, 'Go to the pool of Siloam and wash. I went, I washed, and I see; this is my testimony.'" We who are saved do have a testimony, and we can witness for Christ by our testimony.

6. The Jews did not believe until they had called his parents who said he could speak for himself. No one can give a testimony for another; it is a personal experience.

7. The man was again asked the same question about receiving his sight; he gave the same answer. We only have one testimony.

8. The man asked a question, "Will ye also be his disciple? Or will you follow him?" So whether we give a testimony or preach the gospel, it is always a good idea to make an appeal.

9. Why herein is a marvelous thing that ye know not from whence he is, and yet he hath open my eyes. If this man were not of God, he could do nothing.

10. They cast him out. The message by Paul and Barnabas was rejected by the Jews at Antioch (Acts 13:46); then they turned to the Gentiles. Many times, our messages are also rejected.

11. Jesus heard they had cast him out, found him, and made himself known to him. Jesus is always a present helper in times of need (Psalm 46:1). A thankful recipient (vs. 38), the man said, "Lord I believe," and he worshipped him. May we ever be thankful for our salvation.

Notes:

3 – A Building of God (Funeral)—2 Cor. 5:1–9

"*F*or we know that if our earthly house of this tabernacle were dissolved, we have a building of God, a house not made with hands, eternal in the heavens."

The definition of the Tabernacle. Regarding the physical body, Peter said, "I must put off this tabernacle" (2 Peter 1:13–14).

The explanation of the Tabernacle as it relates to man: man is a triune being of a three-in-one component of spirit, soul, and body. In Luke 1:43–44, Mary said, "My soul doth magnify the Lord, and my spirit hath rejoice in God my Savior." Mary spoke of the three components of man. In 1 Thessalonians. 5:23, the Apostle Paul said, "I pray God your whole spirit and body be preserved blameless unto the coming of our Lord Jesus Christ." Paul spoke of the three components of man.

The function of the three components of man: (1) the spirit is Psalm 42:1–2; 2 Samuel 1:26—the that of intelligence and knowledge (1 Cor. 2:11); (2) the soul is that of emotions, desires, and affection (Soul of Jonathan and David, the love passeth the love of women); and (3) man has self-consciousness. The body as referred to in the text is the Tabernacle or house for the spirit and soul, as all three make up the man and are inseparable during this life. However, at the time of death, the body, our earthly house or this tabernacle, is dissolved (Eccles. 12:7). But there will be a new one. Parliaments dissolve and are replaced, organizations dissolve and are replaced by others, and so we as Christians have a building of God eternal in the heavens to be united with the spirit and soul at the resurrection when God will give a body as it pleases Him (1 Cor.15:38). There are celestial bodies and terrestrial bodies, or heavenly and earthly. To have a celestial body, one must be born again and saved by the blood of the crucified One (John 3:5). There is another that is also eternal, but God does not want anyone to have that one (2 Peter 3:9).

Notes:

4 – Afraid but Where Could I Go?—Joshua 20:1–9

There is a city of refuge.

In the book of Genesis, chapter 12, we read that God called Abram saying "Get thee out of thy country." Abram whose name was changed to Abraham obeyed, went with his wife Sara to the land of Canaan, where he built an altar unto the Lord and called unto the name of the Lord. According to the generations of Abraham, we find Abraham had Isaac and Isaac had Jacob. Jacob, whose name was changed to Israel, had twelve sons. In course of time, they were brought down to Egypt and were afflicted for four hundred years until they cried unto the Lord. God raised up a leader Moses among them, who led them from Egypt to Moab after which Joshua his successor took over and led them to Canaan the Promised Land.

Now we see God's instruction to Joshua to appoint six cities of refuge so that if any one slay another, he could run to one of these cities of refuge. There was no city of refuge before until God gave Joshua the instruction to do so (Joshua 20:1–9).

1. The availability of the city Joshua 20, vs. 4). There were three on the east side of the Jordan and three on the west side.
2. "Until he stand before the congregation for judgment and until the death of the high priest that shall be in those days, then shall the slayer return, and come unto his own city."

    This reminds us of our security in Christ (Romans 8:1; John 5:24) and praise God that Christ our great high priest shall never die. Hebrews 7:23–24 says, "And they truly were many priests, because they were not suffered to continue by reason of death. But this man because he continueth forever hath and unchangeable priesthood."

Notes:

5 – Balaam, the Professing Prophet of God—Numbers 22:1–28

The three B's: Battles, Balak, and Balaam.

The story which lies beyond the actions of Balaam concerns the battles Israel fought and won. In Exodus 20:14–22, Moses requested passage through the land of the Edomites, but the king of Edom refused and promised to fight with Israel, so Israel passed around his territory. In Numbers 21:1–4, King Arad the Canaanite went out and fought against Israel but was defeated. In 21:21–25, Israel made the same request to Sihon, king of the Amorites, as he did to the king of Edom, and though he refused, Israel went to war and defeated the Amorites. Now in chapter 22, we will consider Balak and Balaam:

Balak, the king of Moab, heard Israel was coming his way. He and the Moabites were greatly afraid of them, so he thought of a plan that he hoped would weaken them so that he might have victory over them. Balak sent for Balaam, a prophet from the Midianites, so that he would curse Israel for him.

Now we shall consider the controversial Balaam and his actions.

1. The promise of promotion Numbers 22 vs. 15–17). Balak sent yet again princes more and more honorable with the message to Balaam, saying, "I will promote thee unto very great honor, and I will do whatsoever thou sayest unto me, come therefore, I pray thee, curse me this people."
2. Now therefore, we take note on the error of Balaam, the way of Balaam, and the doctrine of Balaam.

Notes:

6 – Blind, Begging, and Believing—Luke 18:35–43

I have seen people who are blind, people who are mute or dumb, and people who are deaf, but I haven't seen any with all three at the same time. In this story, we have a blind man who was not mute or dumb. He was not deaf or hard of hearing, so he was able to hear the multitude passing by and asked what it meant. They told him that Jesus of Nazareth was passing by. This man had knowledge of Jesus who could give him sight; he saw he had an opportunity to receive his sight, so he cried, "Jesus, thou Son of David, have mercy on me."

As we consider this man in light of our relationship with God, we may take note of:

1. The concern of the man Luke 18 vs. 36). He was in a state of hopelessness.
2. The commitment of the man Luke 18 vs. 43). He followed Jesus, glorifying God.

    This tells us that we have been born in darkness or spiritual blindness, so are we concerned as to our condition before God? Is there carefulness or carelessness on our part? If there is carefulness, then there is hope and satisfaction available to us in Christ Jesus. If we receive Christ as Savior, then we are His disciples, his followers. There is a song which says:

> *Come, contrite one, and seek His grace*
> *Jesus is passing by;*
> *See in his reconciled face;*
> *The sunshine of the sky.*
> *Chorus*
> *Pass... ing by... Pass....ing by*

Hasten to meet Him on the way,
Jesus is passing by today
Pass... ing by... Pass... ing by.

Redemption Song Book #150
by Harper Collins Publishers,
77-85 Fulham Palace Road, London W6-8JB

Notes:

7 – Baptism the Identification with Christ—Romans 6:1–22

What shall we say then? Shall we continue in sin, that grace may abound? God forbid, How shall we, that are dead to sin, live any longer therein? Know ye not, that so many of us as were baptized into Jesus Christ were baptized into his death?

These are questions that deserve answers.

1. The mode of baptism Romans 6 vs. 4). How was it done according to scripture? Jesus went down into the river of Jordan, and after he was baptized, he went up straightway out of the water (Matt. 3:16). "The Ethiopian eunuch commanded his chariot to stand still, and both he and Philip went down into the water, both Philip and the eunuch, and Philip baptized the eunuch. And when they were come up out of the water, the Spirit of the Lord caught away Philip, that the eunuch saw him no more; and he the eunuch went on his way rejoicing" (Acts 8:38–39).

2. Type of offering in Leviticus 1:1–5, a bullock, (vs.3), a lamb (vs. 10), two turtle doves (vs. 14).

   (a) The method of approach—voluntary.

   (b) The measure of appreciation—a bullock, a lamb, or two turtledoves.

   (c) The manner of appropriation—how he was affected by what God has done for him. Our thanksgiving and worship can be likened to these offerings. What do we present to the Lord for delivering us from the bondage of sin to the glorious liberty of fellowship with a risen Christ and the prospect of being with him someday?

Notes:

8 – Before and After—Ephesians 2:2, 11–12; Rom. 12:1–2

*A*ccording this passage, there are three things we can see which present to us the life of a believer: the past, the present, and the future.

1. The conversion of a life now profitable to God: Present. "But God who is rich in mercy, for his great love wherewith he loved us, Even when we were dead in sins, hath quickened us together with Christ (by grace ye are saved) But now in Christ Jesus ye who sometimes were far off are made night by the blood of Christ Ephesians 2: vs 4–6,& 13).

2. The consolation for a life with a present enjoyment and a future hope. Future: verses 7–8 say, "That in the ages to come he might shew the exceeding riches of his grace in his kindness toward us through Christ Jesus. For by grace are ye saved through faith, and that not of yourselves, it is the gift of God, not of works lest any man should boast." And for the future hope, we see in Ephesians 5:27, "That he (Christ) might present it (the church) to himself a glorious church, not having spot or winkle, or any such things but that it should be holy and without blemish." There is a little chorus we used to sing: "The Wages of Sin Is Death":

> *The wages of sin is death*
> *The wages of sin is death*
> *But the gift of God is eternal life!*
> *Through Jesus Christ our Lord.*

Notes:

9 – Chosen, Called, and Commissioned

2 Thessalonians. 2:13–17, cf. Acts 22:11–16; 2 Peter. 3:9; Romans. 10:13–15

The Apostles Paul and Barnabas, while ministering at the local church at Antioch in Syria, were commended to the grace of God for full-time ministry of preaching and teaching the word of God. They being sent forth by the Holy Ghost, went up to Asia Minor, and did the work to which they were commended. In Acts 14:26 we read they returned to the local church that commended them to the ministry and gave a report on their experiences and what the Lord had done as people responded to the gospel. There should be no freelance preachers; we all should have a company or a local church to which we belong even though we are out for six months or more. Also it's very encouraging while you are out to know the local church is praying for you and the ministry.

In Acts 15:36–41 we read:

And some days after Paul said unto Barnabas, Let us go again and visit our brethren in every city where we have preached the word of the Lord, and see how they do. But there they separated themselves and each had a new partner, but both continued their ministries. Now it became Paul and Silas, and Barnabas with John Mark.

While Paul and Silas were at Troas God spoke to them of ministries at Philippi, Thessalonica, Berea, then at Berea Paul was forced to leave Silas and Timothy there and he alone went to Athens, Corinth, Ephesus, then after the uproar at Ephesus Paul went to Macedonia, then back to Troas and then to Jerusalem.

I would like us to consider Paul's ministry to the Thessalonians:

1. The commendation of the saints at Thessalonica (1:9) included their work of faith in that they turned to God from idols, their labor of love to serve the living and true God, and their patience, waiting for His

Son from heaven, whom He raised from the dead, even Jesus, which delivered us from the wrath to come.

2. Chosen by God's sovereign grace; God led the Apostle Paul to bring the Thessalonians the word. Today God has many ways by which His word comes to us, whether by a gospel tract, by a preacher, by someone witnessing to us, by radio or TV, and by different forms of technology.

3. Called by the Gospel; God speaks through His 2 Thess word (. 2:14). "And whosoever will call upon the Lord for salvation will be saved (Romans 10:13). In Acts 6:7, we read many of the priests were obedient to the faith. After we believe on the Lord Jesus Christ and are saved (Acts 16:31), there is:

4. The commission to service (2 Timothy 4:1–2) with the charge and solemn responsibility, including the motivation to respond (Luke 5:17–20) with the call, the concern, and the commitment, then there must be:

   The consistency in our Christian life and service, according to the following exhortations:

   Stand Fast 2 Thess 2:15
   Hold Fast our profession (Heb. 10:23);
   Holding faith and good conscience. 1 Tim. 1:19
   Holding forth the word of life. Phil. 2:16,
   Holding fast the faithful word. 1 Tim. 1.9
   Hold fast till I come Rev. 2:25; and
   The comfort and consolation by God (2 Thess. 2:16).

Notes:

10 – Five Judgments as Recorded in the New Testament

Of the five judgments as recorded in the New Testament, one is past, one is present, and three are for the future. They are as follows:

1. The judgment for sins (John 12:31—33:9, in the past) Jesus said "Now is the judgment of this world: now shall the Prince of the world be cast out. And I, if I be lifted up from the earth, will draw all men unto me. This He said signifying what death He should die." This is the judgment on Christ for our sins. In Isaiah 53:5 we read, "But he was wounded for our transgressions, he was bruised for our iniquities: the chastisement of our peace was upon him, and with his stripes we are healed."

2. The self-judgment of the believer (1 Cor. 11:28–31, in the present) This passage presents to us our preparation in view of communion or the breaking of bread in remembrance of the death, burial, and resurrection of Christ. "But God commendeth His love toward us, in that, while we were yet sinners, Christ died for us" (Rom. 5:8).

3. The judgment seat of Christ (2 Corinthians or 5:10, to come in the future). "For we must all appear before the judgment seat of Christ, that every one may receive the things done in his body, according to that he hath done. Whether it be good or bad. If any man's work abide which he hath built there upon he shall receive a reward. If any man's work shall be burned he shall suffer loss, but he himself shall be saved yet so as by fire." Therefore this judgment is not for salvation but for reward. This judgment is like an award ceremony for how we lived since we have been saved by the blood of the crucified one. Awards will be different for six categories are mentioned in 1 Cor. 3:11–15—gold, silver, precious stone, wood, hay, and stubble. We can also receive crowns:

    1. Faithfulness in service—a crown or righteousness (2 Tim. 4:8)

2. Faithfulness in temptation—a crown of life, (James 1:12)
3. Faithfulness in witnessing—a crown of Rejoicing, (1 Thess. 2:19)
4. Faithfulness in shepherding—a crown of glory (1 Peter 5:4; 1 Corinthians. 9:24–25)

We should be faithful to God with whatever we have and in the best way we can. We may not receive all five, but we can show steadfastness in the journey with its crown incorruptible. We may not have the same strength, talent, and ability, but God will reward us as we yield and make ourselves available to Him. We can think of some of the judges in Israel:

There is a chorus which goes like this:
Shamgar had an ox goad,
David had a sling,
Dorcas had a needle,
Rahab had a string;
Sampson had a jawbone,
Aaron had a rod,
Mary had some ointment,
But they all were used for God.

We can also think of the testimony of three men in the Bible.

The Apostle Paul, who said, "I have fought a good fight, I have kept the faith" (2 Tim. 4:7).

Caleb, who said, "I have wholly followed the Lord" (Joshua 14:6–8).

Saul, Israel's first king said, "I have played the fool (1 Samuel 26:21).

4. The judgment of the nations (Matthew 25:31–46; this comes in the future) This judgment will be during the tribulation, known as the sheep and goats selection by Christ and will include the Jews and Gentiles who will show kindness to Israel as they go through the

tribulation, to be considered as part of the first resurrection to inherit the earth (Rev. 7:4–17). This judgment is future.

5.   The Great White Throne Judgment (Rev. 20:11–15—future and last). "And I saw a great white throne, and him that sat on it, from whose face the earth and the heaven fled away; and there was found no place for them." At that time there will be many who had an opportunity and many even today who still have the opportunity to receive Christ as Savior but fail to trust him, and it may be too late when they would like to do so. *The sad ending is the lake of fire.* This passage is self-explanatory.

Notes:

CHAPTER 2

11 – From Hopelessness to Happiness

Ephesians 2:1-3 and. 2: – 4-13

To introduce this outline, we will start at the second half of Ephesian chapter 2 vs.11–13). There are three groups of people in the world: the Jews, descendants of Abraham; the Gentiles, anyone who is not a Jew; and the church of God, composed of both Jews and Gentiles. The apostle is reminding the Gentile believers as to their state before God in the past.

1. The meaning of our position Ephesian 2 vs. 11–12 cf. vs. 1–3): "That at that time ye were without Christ, being aliens from the commonwealth of Israel, and strangers from the covenants of promise, having no hope, and without God in the world, but now in Christ Jesus ye who sometimes were afar off are made right by the blood of Christ."

2. The method of our salvation Ephesians 2 vs. 4–10): "But God who is rich in mercy for his great love wherewith he loved us, even when we were dead in sins hath quickened us together with Christ, (by grace ye are saved)." A sovereign God by His sovereign grace secured for us a simple plan of salvation, whereby a seeking sinner, through faith in Christ, can freely find true happiness.

3. The mystery of no distinction Ephesians 2 v s.6). In this relationship with God, there is no distinction between Jew and Gentiles (Gal. 5:6; John 3:16). "For ye are all the children of God through faith in Christ Jesus" (Gal. 3:26). We are all a called-out people, called to be saints.

4. The bright hope to a glorious celebration Ephesians 2 vs. 7). "That in the ages to come he might shew the exceeding riches of his grace in his kindness toward us through Christ Jesus, for He shall present His church to himself a glorious church, not having spot or wrinkle, or any such thing, but that it should be holy and without blemish."

Notes:

12 – From the Prospect of Death to the Reality of Life
2 Kings 7:1–16

In chapter 6, verse 24, we read that Benhadad, king of Syria, gathered all his army and invaded Samaria, which brought about a famine in the city of Samaria. In 7:3–8, we read there were four men with leprosy at the gate of Samaria. They couldn't go into the city because of their illness; they had to stay out, put a piece of tape under their nose, and cry unclean so that no one would come near to them because this was a highly contagious disease. They asked themselves a question:

Why sit we here until we die? If we say, we will enter into the city then the famine is in the city, and we shall die there: and if we sit still here we die also. Now therefore come, and let us fall unto the host of the Syrians: if they save us alive, we shall live; and if they kill us, we shall but die.

1. The condition of the men 2nd Kings 7 vs 3). They were sick and helpless and ready to die according to their illness.
2. The concern of the men 2nd Kings 7 vs. 3a). They couldn't remain in that situation; they had to do something about it.
3. The commitment of the men 2nd Kings 7 vs.4). They all decided to do something about their condition and situation. So they asked themselves a question: "Why sit we here until we die? There is no hope; we all are in the same situation, so we can't help each other, and we can't go into the city, so what option do we have?"
4. The conclusion of the men 2nd Kings 7 vs. 4b). "Now therefore come, and let us fall unto the host of the Syrians: if they save us alive, we shall live; and if they kill us, we shall but die." They did not have any assurance that their lives would be saved, but they would take the chance. But by God's grace, they were saved and satisfied.
5. The communication of the men 2nd Kings 7 vs. 9–10). They talked things over as they remembered how they were, and how the people

in the city had nothing to eat. They said, "We do not well, this is a day of good tidings, and we hold our peace." They let the city know of their blessing that the people could go and find the same food they had found.

The application to this as it relates to our state before God is "All have sinned and come short of the glory of God" (Rom. 3:23), and no one can save himself or another; all of us are in the same situation. What could these leprous men try; what could man try to bring about happiness? They could try good works, going to church, good deeds, changing practices, but there is none righteous (Rom. 3:9–12). However, there is someone to turn to—Christ invites us to come to Him for there is full assurance of acceptance and satisfaction. The invitation is: "Come now and let us reason together" (Isaiah 1:18); "Come unto me and I will give you rest" (Matt. 11:28); "and the Spirit and the Bride say come (Rev. 22:17). By coming to Christ, satisfaction and happiness will be realized. After this, what do we do next? Seek to help others find the same satisfaction and happiness we are enjoying in Christ. If not fully engaged in making the richest of God's grace, we should be saying, "We do not well, or we are not doing well. This is a day of good tidings, and we are holding out peace. We must tell others of the satisfaction we have found in Christ."

Notes:

13 – God's Call to Moses and God's Last Call to Pharaoh

Exodus 3:1–20; 4:1–9; 7through–11

M oses watched the sheep of Jethro, his father-in law, who lived in the backside of the desert. "And the angel of the Lord appeared unto him in a flame of fire out of the midst of the bush, and he looked, and behold, the bush burned with fire, and the bush was not consumed. And Moses said, I will now turn aside, and see this great sight, why the bush is not burnt."

1. The circumstances surrounding Moses Exodus 3:1–6). Moses was feeding the flock, and when the Lord saw that he turned aside to see, God called unto him out of the midst of the bush, and said; Moses, Moses. And he said "Here am I."

2. The commission to Moses Exodus 3 vs. 7–10). And the Lord said, "I have surely seen the affliction of my people which are in Egypt, and have heard their cry by reason of their taskmasters, for I know their sorrows. Come now therefore, and I will send thee unto Pharaoh, that thou mayest bring forth my people the children of Israel out of Egypt."

3. The comfort of God to Moses Exodus 3 vs. 11–18). God said unto Moses, "I will be with thee and this shall be a token unto thee that I have sent thee."

4. The challenge of God for Pharaoh King of Egypt, Exodus vs. 18–20). He will only release them when the hand of God is upon him.

5. The complaint to God by Moses (Exodus 4 verse 1). They will not believe me; I am not eloquent (Exodus 4 vs 10).

6. The convincing evidences of God's presence with Moses Exodus 4 vs2–9).

7. The commitment to Moses, the seven "I wills" (Exodus 6:6–8).

    Wherefore say unto the children of Israel, I am the Lord and (1) I will bring you out from under the burdens of the Egyptians, (2) I will rid you out of their bondage (3) I will redeem you with a stretched out arm, and with great judgment (4) I will take you to me for a people (5) I will be to you a God: and ye shall know that I am the Lord your God (6) I will bring you in unto the land concerning the which I did swear to give it to Abraham, to Isaac, and to Jacob; and (7) I will give it you for an heritage, (and God signed the statement). I am the Lord.

8. The contest with Pharaoh, Exodus chapters 7— 11, but Pharaoh lost.

     A Water turns into blood (7:14–19)

     B Frogs in the rivers (8:1–5)

     C Lice upon men and beasts (8:16–19

     D Flies in the homes (8:20–24)

     E Cattle dying in Egypt (9:1–7)

     F Boils breaking out (9:8–12)

     G Hail with fire 9:13–25)

     H Locusts in the coast (10:4–05)

     I Darkness in the land (10:21–23); and finally

     J Death of the firstborn (12:1–13, 29–36).

The compromise of Pharaoh, five of which are:

     A Go, sacrifice in the land (8:25)

     B Go, but not far (8:28)

     C Go, but who shall go (10:8)

     D Go ye that are men (10:11)

     we Go with your little ones, but leave your flock (10:24)

The uncompromising answer by Moses: Moses said, "There shall not be a hoof left, we all will be going men, women children and animals for sacrifices."

Pharaoh had hardened his heart five times, and then God hardened Pharaoh's heart.

Notes:

14 – God Getting Our Attention—Amos 4:1–13

In Exodus 34:6–7 we read, "The Lord, The Lord God, merciful and gracious, longsuffering, and abundant in goodness and truth. Keeping mercy for thousands, forgiving iniquity and transgressions and sins, and that will by no means clear the guilty." This tell us much of the person and character of God as merciful and gracious but also righteous.

In Amos 4:1–13, we can see God getting the attention of the people of Israel by speaking to through the prophet Amos.

1. The insincerity of their worship Amos 4 vs. 4–5). Going to Bethel and practicing worship with an unprepared heart was just going through the motions.
2. The insensitivity of the people to God's chastening's. (Amos 4 vs. 6–11). Despite their experiences with God, five times God said, "And yet have ye not returned to me" (vs. 6, 8–11)? The incoming and swift judgment to them (vs. 12–13). "Prepare to meet thy God, O Israel." This was sure; it was only a matter of time before it would happen.

God is the same yesterday, today, and evermore. However, we see God always making provision that mankind does not experience His judgment. A sovereign God by His sovereign grace hath secured for us a simple plan of salvation, whereby a seeking sinner can find deliverance and peace instead of experiencing the judgment of God.

Notes:

15 – Grace Unlimited—2 Sam. 9:1–13; 2 Cor. 8:9

The Definition of God's Grace

Someone said (a) grace is something for nothing; (b) another said grace is everything for nothing, (c) but another rightly said grace is everything for the undeserving, and this is the right definition of God's grace.

The story which lies behind the above text begins at 1 Samuel 27:1. David said in his heart, I shall now perish by the hand of Saul. And then he went to the land of the Philistines, joined himself to Achish the King of Gath, who gave him a little inland town name Ziglag.

In course of time war broke out in Jezreel between Israel and the Philistine, with David on the enemy side. The war was so fierce that Israel fled to Gilboa where both King Saul and Jonathan his son died in one day. David having received the news of their death lamented over Saul and Jonathan. David had a great love for Jonathan who helped him to escape the wrath of Saul. Jonathan had a son name Mephibosheth, who was five years old when tidings came that both Saul and Jonathan died in the battle at Jezreel, his nurse took him up to run with him when he fell from her and became lame on both feet.

David now being led by God went up to Hebron in Judah. The men of Judah came and anointed David king over Judah. Upon being king, David said "Is there yet any that is left of the house of Saul, that I may show him kindness for Jonathan's sake?" Ziba the servant of Saul said Jonathan hath yet a son but is lame on his feet in Lo-debar, a town in Manasseh. The king sent and fetch him from there, that he might show him the kindness of God for Jonathan's sake, thus granting grace unlimited to the undeserving.

Mephibosheth: The unhealthy beneficiary (vs. 7)
Mephibosheth: The unworthy recipient (vs. 8)

Mephibosheth: The unbroken relationships (vs. 9)

Mephibosheth: The unlimited supplies (vs. 10–12)

Mephibosheth: The untainted appearance (vs. 13)

But God's grace is more far reaching (2 Cor. 8:9).

"Ye know the grace of our Lord Jesus Christ, that though he was rich, yet for your sakes He became poor, that ye through His poverty might be rich." As the songwriter states: "Wandering like a homeless stranger in this world that He had made."

Christ is rich in glory. "O Father, glorify thou me with the glory which I had with Thee before the world was" (John 17:5). Christ the brightness of God's glory (Heb. 1:3).

Christ is rich in power: "All power is given unto Me" (Matt. 11:18). "Even the winds and the waves obey Him (Matt. 8:27).

Christ is rich materially. "The earth is the Lord's, and the fullness thereof" (Psalm 24:1). The cattle upon a thousand hills are his (Psalm 50:10). For by Him were all things created (Col. 1:18). That we might be rich: (a) in Faith (James 2:5); (b) in wisdom (1 Cor. 1:30); and (c) in love and kindness—He has given us the capacity to love and be kind (1 John 4:7; Eph. 4:32).

Notes:

16 – God's Intended Purpose for Mankind—Eph. 1:4, 6

*T*hat we should be holy and without blame before him in love.... That we might be to the praise and glory of his grace.

In the Catholic catechism, we learn that God made us, to know him, to love him, to serve him in this world, and to be happy with him forever in the next. Good, but does man in his natural state meet the intended purpose of God? *No*. What went wrong? And what is the solution to correct the problem? But what is the problem?

In Romans 5:12 we read, "by one man sin entered into the world and death by sin and so death passed upon all men, for all have sinned." In Job 9:33, we find a cry for a solution to the problem of sin. Neither is there any daysman betwixt us that might lay his hand upon us both"." because in Isaiah 64:6 we read, "But we are all as an unclean thing and all our righteousness are as filthy rags." However, in Job 25:4, Bildad, one of Job's friends, asks one of the most important two-part questions in the history of mankind: "How can a man be justified with God or how can he be clean that is born of a woman?" But thanks be to God this question has been answered by the Apostle in Acts 13:38–39:

Be it known unto you therefore, men and brethren, that through this man (Jesus Christ) is preached unto you the forgiveness of sins: And by him all that believe are justified from all things, from which ye could not be justified by the law of Moses but this declaration could not have been made without the death of Christ and the exercise of faith by the person who is declared righteous.

However, when this information was presented in the first century, there was a three-way response, as we see in Acts 17:30–34. Some mocked, some procrastinated by saying we will hear thee again, but some believed, and this is evident today.

Finally, in Acts 13:46, we read that when the apostle Paul and Barnabas preached at Antioch in Asia, some believed and some did not believe. Then

Paul and Barnabas were bold and said, "It was necessary that the word of God should first have been spoken to you: but seeing ye put it from you and judge ourselves unworthy of everlasting life, lo, we turn to the Gentiles."

Notes:

17 – God Is looking for You

Ezekiel 22:30; Isaiah 6:1–6; 1 Sam. 30:1–10; 18:25

The occasion of this verse was due to the situation in Israel as we can see from Ezekiel 22 verses 6–29. Israel was indicted for their disobedience Ezekiel 22 vs. 6–16). They were advised of judgments that would come Ezekiel 22 vs. 17–22). The priests, princes, prophets, and the people were told that their practices were not helping the conditions they were in. Therefore, God is looking for someone to stand for Him. Read Ezekiel 22:30.

God was looking for one who knows their language, custom and practices, one who is prepared in heart, has a burden, and is knowledgeable of God's word and his judgment. He is looking for one to stand in the gap, (the place to give direction) like a traffic policeman; God is look for one whose objectives are so that they do not come into God's judgment. But God said he found none. God is still seeking representatives (Matt. 28:19).

God is calling for you as in Isaiah 6:1–8. This was the year King Uzziah died by intruding in the temple of God to burn incense when leprosy rose up in his forehead before the priests and was hastened out (2 Chron. 26:1, 16–23). This is the year when Isaiah saw the Lord sitting upon a throne, and the seraphims said "Holy, Holy, Holy is the Lord of hosts." Then Isaiah said, "Woe is me, I am undone, I dwell in the midst of a people of unclean lips." "Then flew one of the Seraphims unto me, having a live coal in his hand, which he had taken with the tongs from off the altar, and he laid it upon my mouth, and said, 'Lo, this hath touched thy lips, and thine iniquity is taken away, and thy sin purged. You are qualified.'"

God is calling, "Whom shall I send?" Isaiah said, "Here I am, send me" Isaiah 6 vs. 8).

God is depending on you. See 1 Samuel 30:1–10, 18–25.

David's little inland town Ziklag was burned with fire by the

Amalekites. David inquired of the Lord about going after them, and God gave him the answer. David with his six hundred men came by the brook Besor, where two hundred remained and abided by the stuff while the four hundred went to battle 1st Samuel 30 vs. 8–11). David recovered all. Upon returning, some of the four hundred did not want the two hundred to get equal share of the spoil, but David said they should get the same amount as those who went to battle. We either go to the front lines or stay by the stuff—which? In the words of Paul: "We are laborers together with Him (1 Cor. 3:5–9). No church communicated with Paul (Philippians 4:15–19).

Notes:

18 – God's Provision for a Full Restoration
2 Samuel 14:14–24

The story which lies behind this is due to the sin of Absalom because he murdered his brother Amnon who had committed a serious immoral act against his sister Tamar. Absalom was angry and sought revenge against Amnon for a period of two years. In order that Absalom may find a convenient time for this revenge, he prepared a feast and invited his father King David and his sons. While David did not attend the feast, Amnon did. Absalom had commanded his servants to kill Amnon when he was merry, which they did. With this, Absalom fled to Geshur.

As we consider this in view of man's relationship to God, we can see the incomparable love of God to a world of sinful men.

1. The transgression of Absalom 2nd Samuel 13 vs 28). He plotted and killed his brother Amnon.
2. The separation of Absalom 2nd Samuel 13:37–39). He went to Geshur and remained there for three years.
3. The compassion of David 2nd Samuel 14:2–14). He sent for Absalom whom he loved after receiving words from a wise woman from Tekoah who was coached by Joab, and these are the words which softened the heart of David. "For we must needs die, and are as water spilt on the ground, which cannot be gathered up again; neither doth God respect any person: yet doth he devise means, that his banished be not expelled from him" 2nd Samuel chapter 14 vs.14).
4. The commission to Joab 2nd Samuel 14:21 –22). David sent Joab to bring back Absalom saying, "Go therefore and bring the young man Absalom again."
5. The immediate action by Absalom 2nd Samuel 14 vs.24). As Absalom got the invitation to return, he did not procrastinate; he came immediately.

However, we see David's half-heartedness attempt at forgiveness by not seeing Absalom for two years when he finally received him.

Application: Man has been separated from God because of transgressions, but the invitation has been issued since Christ died for our sins. There is no waiting period for our acceptance: "For the son of man is come to seek and to save that which was lost" (Luke 19:10). "Him that cometh to me I will in no wise cast out" (John 6:37).

Notes:

19 – God's Time Clock—Gal. 4:4–6

*A*t every moment of the day, someone is awaiting the time for some specific reason, for example, high school graduation, marriage, an appointment to a new job and so forth. But we can see the unfolding of God's time for his plan for the salvation of man who sinned against him, according to his eternal purpose that we should be to the praise of his glory (Eph. 3:11).

1. The promise of God's plan. Genesis 3:15 tells us God said the seed of the woman shall bruise the head of the serpent, referring to the victory of Christ by His resurrection.

2. The promise of God's plan confirmed to Abraham. Gen. 12:3 says, "In thy seed shall all the families of the earth be blessed."

3. The person who according to the flesh would be used to fulfill His word. Isaiah 7:14 informs us, "Therefore the Lord himself shall give you a sign; Behold, a virgin shall conceive, and bear a son, and shall call his name Immanuel."

4. The place where God's plan will be brought in effect. Micah 5:2 says, "But thou, Bethlehem Ephratah, though thou be little among the thousands of Judah, yet out of thee shall he come forth unto me that is to be ruler in Israel, whose goings forth have been from of old."

5. The presence of the Savior, according to God's time and God's plan. A long period of time would pass before this would be realized. God would raise up prophets and other events leading up to the presence of the Savior. Prophets like Isaiah, Jeremiah, Haggai, and Malachi; then there was what has been called the 400 years of silence from Malachi to Matthew. During that period there would be unrest, revolts, and rebellions.

In 333 BC, we see the struggles between nations as Syria-Egypt. In 198 BC, Judea was conquered by Antiochus the Great and was put under Syria. Then in 168 BC, Antiochus the Great profaned the temple by offering a sow upon the altar. As a result, there was a revolt by the Maccabees of whom was Mattathias, the first of the Maccabees who tried to free the nation of Israel and restore ancient worship. He was succeeded by his son Maccabaeus who was assisted by four brothers. This is known as the reign of the Maccabees. Then in 165 BC, Judas regained possession of Jerusalem, rededicated the temple, and held the Feast of the Dedication. But there were still struggles with Antiochus and his successors, leading to a civil war.

The civil war was terminated by the Roman conquest of Judea and Jerusalem by Pompey in 63 BC, and in 47 BC, Antipater was made governor of Judea by Julius Caesar, who appointed his son Herod to be governor of Galilee. However, Julius Caesar was murdered, leading to disorder in Judea. This sent to Herod running to Rome where he was appointed king of the Jews, so he returned to Judea and Jerusalem, and he was the King Herod when Jesus was born. He was Herod Antipas who beheaded John the Baptist (Matt. 14:1–10). Then there was Herod Agrippa who killed James the brother of John (Acts 12:1–4); he was invited to listen to the apostle Paul's defense before Governor Festus when he said, "Almost thou persuaded me to be a Christian" (Acts 26:19–29).

Now returning to our text in Gal. 4:4–6 when God's promise of a redeemer would be fulfilled. We see the promise of the coming of Christ, the Person, according to the flesh, by whom he would be coming, the place where he would be coming, and now the presence of His coming (Matt. 2:1)—now when Jesus was born in Bethlehem of Judea in the days of Herod the king. But now we can consider the purpose for which he came.

This is a faithful saying and worthy of all acceptation, that Christ Jesus came into the world to save sinners. (1 Timothy 1:15)

But as many as received him to them gave he power to become the sons of God, even to them that believe on his name. (John 1:12)

And because we are sons God hath sent forth the Spirit, the Holy Spirit, of his Son into our hearts crying Abba father. (Gal 4:6)

Therefore we can sing the song:

Ab-ba father we approach Thee,
In our Savior's precious name,
We Thy children here assembling,
Access to Thy presence claim.
From our guilt His blood has washed us,
Tis thro' Him our souls draw nigh
And Thy Spirit, too has taught us
Ab-ba Father thus to cry.

The Believers Hymn Book #1
by James G Deck sold at John Ritchie Ltd.
Kilmarnock, Scotland

Notes:

20 – God's Provision for Man's Salvation

Luke 14:16–24

In my experiences I have seen many great feasts or banquets and have considered that such events came about by much sacrifice, time, and energy by many. Therefore, those who made such sacrifices are always worthy of our appreciation. In this story we see:

1. The preparation of the man The gospel of Luke 14 vs.16—A great supper).
2. The proclamation of the servants Luke 14 vs. 17; cf. Luke 5:17; Mark 2:5; 2. Tim. 4:1–2)—A message given).
3. The procrastination by the ones invited Luke 14: 18–20—an invitation refused).
4. The persuasion of the people: Luke 14: vs .21–23—A pleading for acceptance of the invitation).
5. The prevention of the people Luke14: vs. 24; cf. Acts 13:44–46—A people who judge themselves unworthy).

    Once again the gospel message:

    From the savior you have heard;
    Will you heed the invitation?
    Will you turn and see the Lord?

    Chorus:
    Come believing! Come believing,
    Come to Jesus! Look and live!
    Come believing! Come believing,
    Come to Jesus look and live.

Redemption Song Book #250
by Harper Collins Publishers, 77-85
Fulham Palace Road, London, W6-8JB

Notes:

CHAPTER 3

21 – Help Wanted—Who Will Go?

Luke 10:1–4; 5:17–26; Mark 2:1–5

I n Luke 9:57, a certain man came to Jesus saying, "I will follow Thee." Jesus said, "The foxes have holes, the birds of the air have nests, but the Son of Man has no place to lay his head." Count the cost, will you follow such a man like this? Jesus said to another, "follow me," but he said, "Lord, suffer me first to go and bury my father." Jesus said, "Let the dead bury their dead, but go and preach the kingdom of God."

Now in Chapter 10, Jesus appointed seventy and sent them two and two before his face into every city and place whither he himself would come, and said, "The harvest truly is great but the laborers are few; pray ye therefore the Lord of the harvest, that he would send forth laborers into his harvest." He did not send them into places where he himself would not go, and we can take note that the vineyard is his and laborers are needed now.

1. The nucleus of the laborers (Luke 10: vs 2). Only seventy were sent in a world of millions at that time.

2. The need of the hour (Luke10:2). How many more are needed, and how must they be gathered? What program must be used to gather them? It is the program of prayer to the Lord of the harvest.

3. The necessity for assistance (Luke 10:2). Laborers are urgently needed; don't wait for the next generation. People are getting old, and people are dying. Therefore, they must be reached in your generation.

4. The nature of the assignment (Luke 10:3). "Go your ways; behold I send you forth as lambs among wolves. The lambs will appear weaker than the wolves, but don't be afraid, for I have sent you, I will be with you" (cf. Acts 13:1–2). The apostle Paul and Barnabas were, commended by the local church but were sent forth by the Holy Spirit.

5. The nearness of the Savior (Luke 10:3–4; cf. Matt. 28:18–19, Heb. 13:5).The songwriter said:

I must have the Savior with me
For I dare not walk alone,
I must feel His presence near me,
And His arms around me thrown.
Chorus.
Then my soul shall fear no more,
Let Him lead me where He will.
I will go without a murmur,
And His footsteps follow still.

Redemption Song Book #9
From Harper Collins Publishers,
77-85 Fulham Palace Road,
London, W6-8JB.

Notes:

22 – Israel's Journey from Egypt to Canaan
Exodus 12—Joshua 11

After spending 400 years in Egypt, God delivered them to go to the Promised Land, and these are some of the places where they stopped.

From Rameses to Succoth with 600,000 men, besides children and a mixed multitude went up also with them; and flocks, and herds, even very much cattle (Exodus 12:37–38).

From Succoth to Etham, and they encamped in the edge of the wilderness (Exodus 13:20). The Lord went before them by day in a pillar of a cloud to lead them the way and by night a pillar of fire to give them light.

From Etham to the Red Sea, where Pharaoh pursued after them, but Moses said, "Fear not; stand still and see the salvation of the Lord." Pharaoh and his horsemen drowned while Israel went on dry ground.

From the Red Sea to the Wilderness of Shur, where they went three days and found no water (Exodus 15:22).

From the Wilderness of Shur to Marah, where they found water, but it was bitter. The people murmured against Moses saying, "What shall we drink?" Moses cried unto the Lord who shewed him a tree, which when he had cast into the water, the waters were made sweet (Exodus 15:23–25).

From Marah to Elim. And they came to Elim where there were twelve wells and seventy palm trees, and they encamped there by the waters. (Exodus 15:27).

From Elim to the Wilderness of Sin between Elim and Sinai. This was the fifteenth day of the second month after they came out of Egypt (Exodus 16:1). Now the whole congregation murmured against Moses, and Aaron said, "Would God we had died by the hand of the Lord in the land of Egypt, for there we had food, but now we are hungry." Then said the Lord unto Moses, "Behold I will rain bread from heaven for you," and the Lord rained manna from heaven (Exodus 16:1–36).

From the Wilderness of Sin to Rephidim, where there was no water, there the people chided with Moses and said, "Give us water that we may drink." Moses cried unto the Lord saying, "What shall I do unto this people" (Exodus 17:1–4)? The Lord said, "I will stand before thee upon the rock in Horeb. Smite the rock, there shall come water out of it." Moses did so, water came out, and the people drank. Then came Amalek and fought with Israel in Rephidim with Joshua as commander in chief. As Aaron and Hur held up Moses' hand, Israel prevailed, but when his hand was down, Amalek prevailed (Exodus 17:8–16). The songwriter said:

> *What various hindrances we meet,*
> *In coming to the mercy seat,*
> *Yet he who knows the worth of prayer,*
> *But wishes to be often there.*
> *Restraining prayer, we cease to fight,*
> *Pray makes the Christian's armour bright,*
> *And Satan trembles when he sees,*
> *The weakest saint upon his knees.*

> *Redemption Song Book*
> *#600 by Harper Collins Publishers,*
> *77-85 Fulham Palace Road, London, W6-8JB.*

Now Jethro, the priest of Median Moses father in law, brought Moses' wife to him and gave him some counsel regarding the work, that he should designate some of the responsibilities to others.

They traveled from Rephidim to Sinai, now three months since they left Egypt. God called Moses up on the mount, God gave Moses a message on His grace to Israel that if they obey his voice, they would be a peculiar people unto Him. The people answered, "All that the Lord hath spoken we will do" (Exodus 19:8). The Lord then gave the Ten Commandments, and in addition 603 laws and instructions (Exodus 20–31). In chapter

25:8, God said "And let them make me a Sanctuary, that I may dwell among them. And there will I meet with them. This is the Tabernacle in the wilderness" (Exodus 25:8–31).

Moses died in the land of Moab, and they buried him in the valley in the land of Moab, over against Beth-peor (Deuteronomy 34:5–8). Then God spoke to Joshua the son of Nun, Moses' minister, saying, "Moses my servant is dead, now therefore arise, go over this Jordan, thou, and all the people, unto the land which I do give them, even to the children of Israel." Joshua then being obedient to the call of God, led the children of Israel to the Promised Land, from the river Jordan to land of Canaan.

Notes:

23 – How did Israel travel with the Tabernacle in the Wilderness?

They traveled with it in the shape of a cross.

NUMBERS CHAPTERS 2 AND 3

FIRST

EAST

JUDAH   74,600

ISSACHAR 54,400

ZEBULUN 57,400

186,400

SECOND, NORTH			THIRD SOUTH	
DAN	62,700	LEVI -22,300	REUBEN	46,500
ASHER	41,500		SIMEON	59,300
NAPHTALI	53,400	ARK	G AD	45, 650
157,600			151,450	

FOURTH

WEST

EPHRAIM   40,500

MANASSEH 32,200

BENJAMIN 35,400

RESPONSIBILITIES

Aaron and his sons shall cover the ark, the table of shewbread, the candlesticks, the golden altar, and the brazen altar (after taking away the ashes). The Kohathites under the directions of Eleazar, the son of Aaron, shall carry these items.

The Gershonites under the direction of Ithamar, the son of Aaron, shall carry the curtains of the Tabernacle and the Tabernacle of the congregation.

The Merarites under the direction of Ithamar, the son of Aaron, shall carry the boards, bars, pillars, and sockets of the Tabernacle. All carriers must be thirty years to fifty years old (Numbers 4).

This we can call maximum security for the Tabernacle, being in the center with 603,550 men around it, like an aircraft carrier with four destroyers surrounding it.

Notes:

24 – Numbering of the Children of Israel in the Wilderness of Sinai and in the Plains of Moab near Jericho

SINAI-MOAB DIFFERENCES

Tribes	Sinai-Numbers 1	Moab-Numbers 26	Differences.
Reuben	46,500	43.700	- 2,770
Simeon	59,300	22,200	- 37,100
Gad	45,650	40,500	-5,150
Judah	74,600	76,500	+1,900
Issachar	54.400	64,300	+9,900
Zebulun	57,400	60,500	+3,100
Ephraim	40,500	32,500	-8,000
Manasseh	32,200	52.700	+20,500
Benjamin	35,400	45,600	+10,200
Dan	62,700	64,400	+1,700
Asher	41,500	53,400	+11,900
Naphtali	53,400	45,400	-8,000
Total	603,550	601,730	-1,820
Levi	22,300	23, 000	+700

Notes:

25 – Jesus Anointed by Mary in View of His Death

Matt. 6:6–13; Mark14:3–9; John12:1–8

Where did Mary anoint the feet of Jesus? In the house of Simon the leper, in the town of Bethany, the same place where Mary, Martha, and Lazarus lived. According to the notes by C. I. Scofield, there are six Marys in the gospels, but this one was the sister of Martha and Lazarus, neighbors to Simon the leper, in the town of Bethany. Martha as usual loved serving (cf. Luke 10:38–42).

What was going on in the house of Simon the leper? A supper in honor of Jesus. "Then Jesus six days before the Passover came to Bethany, where Lazarus was which had been dead, whom he (Jesus) raised from the dead" (John 12:1). This is in reference to what had happen in chapter 11. Therefore it is easy to say this dinner was in honor of Jesus and His work in raising Lazarus from the dead.

Who were the invited guests? Jesus, His disciples, Mary, Martha, and Lazarus.

Who were those uninvited guests? Many people who came to see Lazarus, whom Jesus raised from the dead (John. 12:9).

What Mary did in view of the death Christ? She came (this implies it was not in her house, but in the house of Simon the leper for she came to the house) with an alabaster box of ointment, very costly and poured it on the head of Jesus, that was the way of anointing in the past, ref: Lev. 8:10–12, 2 Samuel 2:4, she wiped the feet of Jesus with her hair, that which was her glory, 1 Cor. 11:15. Then the house was filled with the odor.

I was at an eightieth birthday party where all guests were dressed up with many fragrances of perfume and cologne, and there the whole room was filled with the aroma of the combination of all these perfumes. This reminded me of the house at Bethany.

What was the reaction of the disciples, particularly Judas? Indignation

Matt. 26:8, Mark 14:4, John 12:4. "To what purpose is this waste, this might have been sold for three hundred pence and given to the poor." From this, we see Mary the worshipper and Judas the criticizer, but Jesus was the Justifier; he said to let her alone—"this is an anointing in view of my death, burial and resurrection."

This also tells us of some people who do not know the meaning of worship to the Lord.

Notes:

26 – Life's Greatest Questions
Isaiah 53:6; 1 Peter 2:25

1. To what have we been compared? Sheep that have gone astray. However, if we received Christ as our Savior, we have returned, not being astray anymore Isaiah 53:6, 1 Peter 2:25.

2. What has been done that made the transfer effective? Romans. 5:8, cf. 1 Peter 2:24?

3. What must we do Acts 3:19? Repent and be converted that our sins may be blotted out, and we will become sinners saved by the grace of God.

4. What is expected of me?

   I must not walk as other Gentiles walk (Eph. 4:17–25).
   I must not walk in the counsel of the ungodly (Psalm. 1:1).
   I must walk circumspectly (Eph. 5:15).
   I must walk worthy of the Lord (Col. 1:10).
   I must walk in love (Eph. 5:1–2).

5. Having returned to the shepherd and bishop of our souls, what kind of shepherd is he?

   Jesus the good shepherd (John 10:11).
   Jesus the great shepherd (Heb. 13:20).
   Jesus the chief shepherd (1 Peter 5:4).

   There is a chorus which said:

   > *Just like a wandering sheep we all have gone astray,*
   > *Just like a wandering sheep we have turned to our own way,*
   > *But in Isaiah we read, in chapter 53,*
   > *God has laid upon Christ our iniquity.*

Notes:

27 – Lost and Found, Part 1: The Lost Sheep

Luke 15:1–7

In Luke 15, we read of three parables spoken by our Lord during his public ministry, and they all speak of the Triune God: (1) The lost sheep: Jesus coming to save us; (2) The lost coin: The Holy Spirit illuminating our minds to see Christ on the cross; and (3) The lost son; the Love of God to us. All three parables speak of being lost but found and the joy that is being expressed after that which was lost was found.

In this study, we shall consider the parable of the Lost Sheep, its relationship to its owner, its separation from its own, and the protection by its owner.

1. The preciousness of the sheep to the man Luke 15 vs. 4; cf. John 3:16). The sheep was precious to the man; the sheep was not aware as to how precious it was to the man. The man knew, so we can say lost but loved.

2. The man pursued the sheep Luke 15 vs. 4. He went where the sheep was; we are not told how difficult the road was, and we would probably not understand. But he went to the end that the sheep might be found cf. Phil. 2:5–8, 1 Peter 1:10–11. We can think of a line in a song, "Although the road be rough and steep, I'll go to the desert to find my sheep."

3. The protection of the sheep. He put it on his shoulders, not one shoulder that it may fall off, but both shoulders, well protected cf. Heb. 10:27–28; 1 Peter 1:5. This speaks of the eternal security of the child of God.

4. The pleasure with the sheep vs. 6. He called together his friends and neighbors saying; Rejoice with me, I have found my sheep which was lost. It's not lost anymore; it has been found. By whom? By the man who went after it cf. Jude 24, Eph. 5:27.

This parable Jesus spoke presents to us our relationship with God; for through the sin of Adam, we all have found ourselves in a lost state as to fellowship with a holy God. But Jesus came to bring us back to God, and he went all the way to the cross and died for our sins. By putting our trust in Him, we shall be found. The road was rough and steep, but He went all the way that we might be found.

Notes:

28 – Lost and Found, Part 2: The Lost Coin

Luke 15:8–10

*E*ither what woman having ten pieces of silver, if she lose one piece doth not light a candle, and sweep the house, and seek diligently till she find it?, and when she hath found it she calleth her friends and her neighbors together saying, Rejoice with me; for I have found the piece which I had lost.

1. The preciousness of that one piece of coin Luke 15 vs. 8. One may say but she still had nine pieces left, so why worry about the one piece that was lost? We see each piece was precious to her.
2. The consciousness of that one piece that was lost. She knew she could not find it without light, for all around was darkness. It was imperative that a light be present, so she lit a candle, the only light available.
3. The brightness of that candle. She did not need another light; that one candle was sufficient to meet the need.
4. The happiness of the woman when she recovered her lost coin. "She calleth her friends and her neighbors together to rejoice with her." All of these have presented to us how far we have been driven from God as a result of sin. In Col. 1:13 we read, "who hath delivered us from the power of darkness and hath translated us into the kingdom of his dear Son? How did it happen? Christ died for our sins, but no man cometh unless the Spirit draw him. How did that happen?

In Joel 2:28, God said I will pour out my Spirit upon all flesh, meaning every one born in this world would be affected by the Holy Spirit. In John 16:7 Jesus said:

It is expedient for you that I go away, for if I go not away, the comforter or the Holy Spirit will not come unto you, but if I depart I will send him unto you. And when he is come, he will reprove the world of sin, and of righteousness and of judgment.

What is the work of the Holy Spirit, first he illuminates, shining into our hearts Galatians 4:6, giving us an impulse as to our need of a Savior and convicting us of sin, of righteousness, and of judgment. Then upon our positive response, the Holy Spirit dwells within us. We are guided by the Holy Spirit and we receive the enablement to glorify God John 16:7–14. This happened to the 3,000 souls who responded to Peter's preaching in Acts 2:16–17, when he quoted Joel 2:28, speaking of the Holy Spirit referred to in the Old Testament. "Now we are no more children of darkness, but children of light: 1 Thess. 5:5.

Notes:

29 – Lost and Found, Part 3: The Lost Son

Luke 15:11–24

And he said; A certain man had two sons. And the younger of them said to his father, Father, give me the portion of goods that falleth to me. And he divided unto them his living. And not many days after the younger son gathered all together, and took his journey into a far country, and there he wasted his substance with riotous living. Luke 15:11–13

1. The perfect relation of the son vs. 11–12. We believe there were the father, the mother and two sons, the boy was first at home with his brother (family relationship and fellowship). And this is a picture of man's original relationship with God by creation Gen. 1:27, Eccl. 7:29.

2. The undesirable separation of the son vs. 13. The boy left home; how sad it was to see him gone. We read in Eccl. 7:29 that God created man upright. Had Adam and Eve been obedient to God, sin would not separate man from God; with this we see man going away from the garden Gen. 3:24. How sad. In Isaiah 59:2 God said to Israel, "your iniquities have separated between you and your God."

3. The right intention of the son Luke 15 vs. 14–16. When he realized his condition, he was feeding swine and eating their food for no man gave unto him. The friends he had were those who would say when you have we have; when we have, you do not have.

4. The unwavering resolution of the son Luke 15 vs. 17–19 "And when he came to himself he said I will arise and go to my father." He now repented of his sins and planned to return to the home, but he did not know whether he would be received.

5. The immediate action by the son Luke 15 vs. 20–21. And he arose and came to his father, he acknowledged his sin and made his confession. The way of acceptance and forgiveness is by the acknowledgment of our sins.

6. The unreserved reception of the son Luke 15 vs. 20b–24. While the boy was not sure of his acceptance, the father was more than anxious to receive his son. He said to his servant "Bring forth the best robe, put a ring on his hand, and shoes on his feet, And bring hither the fatted calf, and kill it, and let us eat and be merry." And they began to be merry but we do not read of an end to the celebration.

This is a picture of man's relationship with God. Man lost the good fellowship with God and is in a state of depravity from God. God is waiting on us to return to Him.

When we come to ourselves and we make a resolution to come to him, we must take an immediate action by receiving Christ as our Savior. Then we are more than welcome to be received by a Holy God. Jesus said in John 6:37 "him that cometh to me I will in no wise cast out." What the boy got: (1)The best robe—we shall be clothed with a robe of righteousness; (2) A ring on his hand—as a ring do not have any evidence as to where it is joined, so with the believer, there is an unending relationship, there is the eternal security of the believer, John 10:27–28; (3) shoes on his feet—God has given us protection from defilement, for sin shall not have dominion over us Romans 6:14; and (4) the fatted calf with a party of which we do not read of its ending. There is joy in the presence of the angels of God over one sinner that repenteth.

There is a song which said:

> *When a sinner comes as a sinner may,*
> *There is joy. There is joy;*
> *When He turns to God in the gospel way,*
> *There is joy, there is joy.*
> *Chorus;*
> *There is joy among the angels,*
> *And their harp with music ring,*

When a sinner comes repenting,
Bending low before the king.

Redemption Song Book #461
Harper Collins Publishes,
77-85 Fulham Palace Road, London W6-8JB

Notes:

30 – Making a Difference by a Surrendered life to God

Neh. 1:1–9;, 2:11–20;, 4:6;, 19–23;, cf: Jeremiah 25:1–10; Daniel 9:1–2; Ezra 1:1–4

"The world has yet to see what God can do, with one man wholly committed to Him" (D. L. Moody".")

This Bible study on the above-mentioned chapters and verses refers to God's warning to the tribe of Judah, their lack of response to His messages by the prophets, and the consequences they experienced, but by His grace, their restoration was a testimony for Him. In Jeremiah 25:1–10, we read that God raised up prophets who gave instructions and warnings to the people of Judah and the inhabitants of Jerusalem for twenty-three years. Because of their failure to respond, God allowed Nebuchadnezzar king of Babylon to come and take them as captives to Babylon for seventy long years. But when Nebuchadnezzar's heart was lifted up and his mind hardened in pride, he was deposed from his kingly throne, and they took his glory from him Daniel 5:20. Belshazzar his son then reigned in his stead. Belshazzar who did not humble his heart, but lifted up himself against the Lord of heaven, was then slain Daniel 5:22–23, 30. This brought to an end the Babylonian Empire, (first world empire), leading to the establishment of the Medo-Persian Empire, (second world empire), under the leadership of Cyrus king of Persia and Darius king of Medes.

In Ezra chapter 1, we read that Cyrus king of Persia in the first year of his reign, made a proclamation that the Jews in captivity can now go back to Jerusalem and rebuild the Temple. Under the leadership of Zerubbabel, they returned, built the temple and established worship. About fourteen years afterward, Nehemiah came up with a company and built the walls around the city, but how was it built? Nehemiah chapters 1, 2, 3, and 4 will let us know.

1. The coming of Hannani from Neh. 1:1–3:

    The words of Nehemiah the son of Hackaliah. And it came to pass in the month Chisleu in the twentieth year, as I was in Shushan the palace. That Hanani, one of my brethren came, he and certain men of Judah: and I asked them concerning the Jews that had escaped, which were left of the captivity and concerning Jerusalem. And they said unto me. The remnant that are left of the captivity that are in the province are in great affliction and reproach. The wall of Jerusalem also is broken down, and the gates thereof are burned with fire.

2. The Concern of Nehemiah—1:4

    "And it came to pass, when I heard these words, that I sat down, and wept, and mourned certain days, and fasted, and prayed before the God of heaven." Notice his action after hearing of the condition. He wept, He mourned, He fasted, and He prayed.

3. The confession of Nehemiah—1:5–7

    He associated himself with the sins of the people, and he acknowledged their transgressions, which brought them to the present situation.

4. The Comfort of Nehemiah—1:8–9

    Nehemiah saw not only their sins, but their acceptance by God if they would return unto Him. He would gather them.

5. The viewing of Nehemiah—2:11–16

    I came to Jerusalem and was there three days. And I arose in the night, I and some few men with me. And I went out by night by the gate of the valley, even before the dragon well, and to the dung port, and viewed the walls of Jerusalem which were broken down, and the gates thereof were consumed with fire.

Nehemiah went quietly. It was a private meditation, no loud noise, no alarm as to what he will do, and he made complete assessment of the situation.

6. The vision of Nehemiah— 2:17–18

Then I said unto them, Ye see the distress that we are in, how Jerusalem lieth waste, and the gates thereof are burned with fire. Come, and let us build up the wall of Jerusalem, that we be no more a reproach." Nehemiah reflected on the past, contemplated on the present, and anticipated as to what the future can be, he called unto the people to build. "Come, and let us build up the wall of Jerusalem, that we be no more a reproach: Let us rise up and build, so they strengthened their hands for the work.

7. The victory by Nehemiah—4:6, 10–23. "So we built the wall; and all the wall was joined together unto the half thereof: For the people had a mind to work."

APPLICATION

This study present to us a picture of the church of our Lord Jesus Christ today and a need for a heart-cry for revival:

(1) Nehemiah had knowledge on the condition of Jerusalem. Do we fully know of the condition of our churches today? Do we make inquiry so that we can know how to pray?

(2) When Nehemiah learned of the condition, what was his reaction? He wept, he mourned, he fasted, and he prayed. When we know of our local churches or when we learn of other churches how some Christians are careless, have a lack of motivation to witness for Christ, and have little interest for attending the weekly prayer meetings and Bible studies, while people are dying in their sins and

going to a lost eternity, what is our reaction? Do we weep? Mourn? Fast and pray? Do we have a heart-cry for a revival in our day?

(3) Nehemiah gave encouragement on the grace of God. Nehemiah 1:8–9 states, "If ye transgress I will scatter you, if ye turn unto me I will gather you," There is no individual Christian or church that God cannot and will not revive.

(4) Nehemiah made a call: "Come let us build" 2:17. The people said "Let us rise up and build" 2:18. With this Bible study, we are saying to you: come let us build. Could you say, "Let us rise up and build"?

(5) Whereas Nehemiah and the people experienced great opposition— chapters 4–5—the work was completed in fifty-two days Nehemiah 6:15–16. The Temple was built and completed in seven years Ezra 6:15.

Notes:

CHAPTER 4

31 – Man's Relationship to and Fellowship with God

"For all have sinned and come short of the glory of God" Romans 3:23. This text is inclusive, universal, and final; none is exempt.

How did we get in this state and condition before a Holy God? "Wherefore as by one man sin entered into the world, and death by sin, and so death passed upon all men, for all have sinned. Romans 5:12".

"How then can man be justified or made right with God? This was a question asked by Bildad, one of Job's so-called friend Job 25:4. The answer is given by the apostle Paul and Barnabas Acts 13:38–39. Be it known unto you therefore men and brethren, that through this man (Jesus) is preached unto you the forgiveness of sins, and by him all that believeth are justified from all things, from which ye could not be justified by the law of Moses."

"God commendeth His love toward us, in that while we were yet sinners Christ died for us Romans. 5:8". Because we can do nothing that would meet God's righteous demand for the remission of our sins, Christ died for us, was buried, and the third day rose again.

What must we do then to be justified before God?

1. We must accept the Bible as the inspired word of God, and what it says to us is true, what it says of God is true, what it says of the blessings offered to us are true, and the judgment it speaks of that will fall on all who reject God's offer of mercy is also true.

2. We must acknowledge the fact that we can do nothing by ourselves, by another, or by following a creed or teaching which does not teach that Jesus Christ came into the world in human form as a child Heb. 2:14, Acts 17:29–31, Acts 4:12.

3. We must believe now and receive Christ as our Savior; there are names for us known to be: believers Acts 5:14; Christians Acts 11:26; disciples Acts 6:1; saints Romans 1:7; and soldiers 2 Timothy 2:3.

Notes:

32 – Ministry from the Book of Philemon

1. The character of the Apostle Paul vs. 1–2.
   - (a) A prisoner of Jesus Christ Ephesians 3:1, 4:1. He was obligated to God and separated unto the gospel of God Romans 1:1.
   - (b) A laborer 1 Cor. 3:9. For we are laborers together with God.
   - (c) A soldier 2 Timothy 2:3. Engaged in warfare.

     We also are prisoners of Christ, laborers with God, and servants of righteousness Rom. 6:18.

2. The character of Philemon 4–7. His love and faith to the Lord and the saints. The communication of that love and faith, causing the bowels of the saints to be refreshed or the saints being edified and encouraged Philemon 7.

3. The character of Onesimus vs. 8–11. He was unprofitable; the time he spent with Philemon was that of tolerance, for he was unprofitable to him. But his departing was for a season as he was saved through the ministry of the apostle Paul at Rome. For it is written of Onesimus that he was a slave of Philemon, a Christian of Colossae; he robbed his master and fled to Rome. There he became a convert through the ministry of the apostle Paul, a prisoner at Rome, who sent him back to Philemon with this letter or recommendation for acceptance by Philemon.

4. The commendation of Onesimus vs. 12–21. Paul gave his commendation for reception, commendation as a brother beloved, and commendation with indemnification. The apostle Paul took responsibility for his behavior and said, "If he hath wronged thee, or oweth thee ought, put that on mine account" vs. 18.

Notes:

33 – Message on Prayer—Luke 18:1–8

1. Luke 18:1 And he Jesus spake a parable unto them to this end, that men ought always to pray and not to faint.

   A parable is an earthly story with a heavenly meaning, or a photo of the real thing. Men ought always to pray. The word *men* was used in generic terms, meaning men women and children (mankind). (1) Who must pray, mankind; (2) Why pray, there are needs Luke 11:5–8; (3) When to pray—always Luke 18:1; (4) How to pray? With all prayer, without ceasing 1 Thess 5:17; Eph. 6:18.

2. What is the method of prayer? Luke 11:1–4 The disciples said Lord teach us to pray as John taught his disciples, Jesus gave the method of prayer; the Lord's prayer is in John 17.

3. What are the divisions in the method of prayer?
   (a) Adoration—Exalting the Lord.
   (b) Thanksgiving—giving thanks for answered prayers Luke 17:15–19.
   (c) Confession—acknowledging our sins and asking God to forgive us Psalm 51; cf. Psalm 23:3.
   (d) Supplication-Making request to God for things that are both personal/collective; Mark 6:11, 1 Chr. 4:9–10.
   (e) Intercession—making request to God for things or places other than ourselves. Gen. 18, Abraham for Lot in Sodom.

4. The assurance of answer to prayers—Luke 11:9–10, A S K—Ask, Seek, Knock.

5. Examples of answered prayers by God's servants
   Gen. 24:12–15—Abraham's servant, And it came to pass, before he had done speaking, that, behold, Rebekah came out, who was born

to Bethuel, son of Milcah, the wife of Nahor, Abraham's brother with her pitcher upon her shoulder.

Daniel—Dan. 9:20. And while I was speaking and praying and confessing my sin and the sin of my people Israel, and presenting my supplication before the Lord my God for the holy mountain of my God.

Jabez—1 Chron. 4:9–10. And Jabez called on the God of Israel, saying Oh that thou wouldest bless me indeed, and enlarge my coast, and that thy hand might be with me, and that thou wouldest keep me from evil, that it may not grieve me, And God granted him that which he requested. There we see the request of Jabez, the reliance of Jabez, and the reward to Jabez.

6. The joy of prayer—Gen. 24. A Bride for Isaac. The deliverance of Peter from prison Acts 12:1–17.

7. The revelation by prayer—Dan. 9:20–27 (prophecies of end times).

8. Deliverance by prayer—Isaiah 36, 37 and the threats from the king of Assyria Isa. 36:4–9; the prayer of Hezekiah Isa. 37:14–20; the message from the prophet Isaiah (Isaiah 37:21–35); the fall of Sennacherib Isa. 37:26–38.

9. The moving of the heart by prayer Neh. 2. 4–6. The Persian king asked Nehemiah, "For what dost thou make request? So I prayed to the God of heaven, a short prayer." Request granted.

10. The encouragement to prayer—prevailing prayer. Jacob said I would not let you go except thou bless me Gen 32:24–26. Persevering prayer 1 Thess. 5:17.

11. The group and individual for prayer, by the elders James 5:14; by the Church Acts 12:5; and by the individual 1 Samuel 1:13. The songwriter said:

> *Restraining prayer we cease to fight,*
> *Prayer makes the Christian's Armour bright,*
> *And Satan trembles when he sees,*
> *The weakest Saint upon his knees.*

Redemption Song Book #600
Harper Collins Publishers,
77-85 Fulham Palace Road, London W6- 8JB

Notes:

34 – Overview on the Book of Acts

Chapter 1: The post-resurrection ministry of Christ, the promise of the Holy Spirit, the power by the Holy Spirit that would enable his disciples and all who put their faith in him in the years to come to be witnesses for Him.

Chapter 2: The Day of Pentecost (one of the seven feast days observed by Israel fifty days after the Passover) The coming of the Holy Spirit and the beginning of the Church Age.

Chapter 3: The healing of the lame man at the Beautiful Gate of the Temple. Peter's message to the Jews regarding their treatment of Christ, "they killed the Prince of Life."

Chapter 4: The first persecution of the apostles, Peter and John. Peter's address before the Sanhedrin or council. With the boldness of Peter and John, they took knowledge that they had been with Jesus.

Chapter 5: The deceptive action of Ananias and Sapphira by misrepresentation of money they received for their property. God's immediate judgment upon them for lying to the Holy Spirit.

Chapter 6: The election of the first deacons, confusion in the early church, and the persecution which brought Stephen before the council.

Chapter 7: Stephen's message on the history of Israel, and how Moses said, "A Prophet shall the Lord your God raise up unto you of your brethren, like unto me, him shall ye hear." Acts 7;37

Chapter 8: The ministry of Philip the evangelist to the city of Samaria and the conversion of the Ethiopian Eunuch.

Chapter 9: The conversion of the Apostle Paul on the Damascus road. Now he preaches the faith which he once destroyed Gal. 1:23.

Chapter 10: The conversion of Cornelius at Caesarea, bringing Gentiles into the church.

Chapter 11: Peter in his ministry vindicated the truth that now Gentiles are included into the church of Christ. For He is our peace who hath made both one, and hath broken down the middle wall of partition between us Eph. 2:14.

Chapter 12: The fifth persecution—Peter, having been arrested, was kept in prison. The power of prayer by the church: "But prayer was made without ceasing by the church unto God for him." Acts 12:5 We must encourage one another to attend the weekly prayer meetings.

Chapter 13: The exercise of heart for missionary work, the separation by God for this work, the sensitivity of the local church to the calling of his servants to that work. The commendation by the local church of the ones whom God called, and the obedience of the apostle Paul and Barnabas to the calling of God.

Chapter 14: The ministry of the apostle Paul and Barnabas at Asia Minor, including Iconium, Derbe, Lystra, and so on. The recognition and ordination of elders (plural) in every church. Having prayed with fasting, they commended them to the Lord on whom they believed. After this they returned to the church at Antioch in Syria, from whence they were commended or sent out and gave report of their mission.

Chapter 15: Certain men came down from Judae and taught the people that they must keep the law of Moses to be saved. Then the church at Antioch in Syria sent Paul and Barnabas to a historical conference at Jerusalem about the matter. At that conference they received instructions, which were sent out to all local churches as to the requirement for salvation.

Chapters 16–19: Timothy became an associate to the Apostle Paul in the ministry at Asia Minor. From there, Paul received a vision from God for ministry in Europe, to such places as Philippi, Thessalonica, Berea, Athens, Corinth, and Ephesus. This led to the conversion of the Philippian jailor Acts 16:30–31.

Chapters 20–21: After the uproar at Ephesus recorded in chapter 19 over the doctrinal dispute concerning the goddess Diana, Paul would make his last visit to Jerusalem where he would be arrested. He traveled through Macedonia until he arrived at Troas. At Troas we see the practice or the breaking of Bread, or the communion, that on the first day of the week, in obedience to the Lord Jesus Christ, when He said, This do in remembrance of me. It is fitting to see it was on the first day of the week so that remembrance covers the death of Christ, the burial of Christ, and the Resurrection of Christ, who was seen resurrected on the first day of the week. Also, the Holy Spirit came on the Day of Pentecost, which is on the first day of the week, which is so meaningful when we meet on Sundays.

Leaving Troas Paul traveled to Miletus, and from Miletus he called for the elders at Ephesus and said to them in chapter 20, verse 28, "Take heed therefore unto yourselves, and to all the flock, over the which the Holy Ghost hath made you Overseers or Elders or Bishop, to feed the church of God which he hath purchased with his own blood." How then one is made an overseer, elder or bishop—by the Holy Ghost and being evident of spiritual gifts, then recognized and pointed out by the local church that is sensitive to the calling by the Holy Spirit.

Chapters 22–28: At Jerusalem Paul gave his testimony, he made known his right to due process and defended his cause for which he was arrested. "Of the hope and resurrection of the dead I am called in question. Acts 23:6." This brought a division in the Council, for the Pharisees believed in the resurrection, while the Sadducees did not believe in the resurrection. With this uproar, Paul might have been pulled in pieces but was rescued by the chief captain, leading to him going to Caesarea to Governor Felix, who heard the message of the faith in Christ, who then said, Go thy way for this time, when I have a convenient season I will call for thee. Felix then was not governor anymore, so Paul had the opportunity to meet Governor Festus and King Agrippa with his wife Bernice, who said, Almost thou persuades me to be a Christian. As they wanted Paul to return to Jerusalem for trial, Paul appeal unto Caesar at Rome. Now Paul would go to Rome with an experience of many dangers.

Notes:

35 – Preparation for His Coming

Matt 25:1–13

In recent times, we have been hearing of many speculations and date setting regarding the coming of Christ for his church to be followed by the Great Tribulation, after the rapture of the church, but little is said regarding preparation for his coming. Some years ago, a brother visited our church, and many times in his message, he would say "The Lord is coming very soon, so you must be ready." In the Lord's message in Matt. 24, we have a list of upcoming events, which include the Great Tribulation, what will happen during that time, and what will happen after that time. These does not apply to the church, for the church would already have been raptured, but anyone, Jew or Gentile alike, who will not been raptured on the basis of their failure to acceptance of Christ as their savior before He comes for His church would be subject to these experiences.

In Matt. 25 we find a continuation of chapter 24 with the word. Then, we find the parable of the ten virgins; five were wise and five were foolish. We take note that they were all virgins, and they all had lamps. The wise took oil in their lamps, but the foolish took no oil in their lamps. While the Bridegroom tarried, they all slumbered and slept. Author William McDonald said in his book *The Believers Bible Commentary*, "The wise virgin represent true disciples of Christ in the tribulation; The foolish virgins represents those who profess to hold the Messianic hope, but who have never been converted, The Bridegroom is Christ in His second coming, known as the revelation of Christ, when He will come to set his earthly kingdom."

At mid-night the announcement was made: "Behold the Bridegroom cometh, go ye out to meet him." They all arose to meet the bridegroom, and they all trimmed their lamps. The only difference is that the foolish did not have oil in their lamps, so they thought they would ask the wise for some. The wise said not so, lest there be not enough for us and you, but go ye rather to them that sell and buy for yourselves. In other words, what we have is nontransferable; we hear these words many a time, and they are non-transferrable. The foolish were intelligent enough to go and seek their own, but as the watch word says "Time and tide waits on no man." There was not enough time for them to go and come back and still meet the Bridegroom, for when they came back the door was shut. The foolish missed their opportunity to meet the Bridegroom—how sad.

While these events will be fulfilled at a later date, there is a present application regarding man's salvation. In 2 Cor. 6:2 we read, "Behold now is the accepted time, behold now is the day of salvation," and this verse refers to our present salvation and future hope as we accept Christ as Savior. Then we will have the Holy Spirit who is not transferrable.

Notes:

36 – Returning to First Place
Isa. 55:6–11

This scripture said, seek ye the Lord while he may be found, call upon Him while He is near vs. 6, Call upon Him while He is near; this means there will come a time when the Lord may not be found, and for this reason we must seek him now. In Revelation 20:11 we read, "And I saw a great white throne, and him that sat on it, from whose face the earth and the heaven fled away and there was found no place for them." This means that when he could have been found, they did not seek him, and now it's too late. When he should have been called upon for salvation, he was not called upon. Behold now is the accepted time, behold now is the day of salvation 2 Cor. 6:20.

Let the wicked forsake his way, and the unrighteous man his thoughts: and let him return unto the Lord, and he will have mercy upon him; and to our God, for he will abundantly pardon vs. 7. Whenever we use the word *return*, it means that we were once there and should come back to the same place; for example, one may have been at a doctor and he might have said return in two weeks or a month, then this person needs to return to him.

By creation, man was with God, but things went wrong in the Garden of Eden; Why? Because of departure from the Lord. God created man upright Gen. 1:27; Eccl. 7:29, but we see in Gen. 3:24, Isaiah 59:2, and Romans 5:12 there has been a change. Therefore there is:

1. A call unto the Lord while he may be found vs. 6–7. There are many voices today, but this call is unto the Lord, the one to whom we all are answerable to.
2. A call from our thoughts vs. 8. Many times we have thoughts that we may be reconciled to God, sometimes sincere but sometimes sincerely wrong. In 2 Kings 5, we read of Naaman, captain of the host of the Syrian army, who was afflicted with leprosy, a highly contagious

disease. He was sent by the king of Syria to the king of Israel to be healed, but the king of Israel thought he was provoked by the king of Syria. Then Elisha the prophet said, let him come now to me and he shall know that there is a prophet in Israel. When Naaman came, Elisha sent a message to him saying, go and wash in Jordon seven times and thou shall be clean, but Naaman was upset and said I thought he would come out and call on the name of the Lord and strike his hand over the place and recover the leper. Naaman had his thoughts, but he had to forsake his thought and go and dip in Jordon seven times to be healed. If we have any other thoughts to be saved from the wrath of God other than that which we find in John 3:16 and Acts 4:12, we must forsake them.

3. A call unto the words of a sovereign God vs. 9–11. God's word will not return to him void; His plans and purposes will be fulfilled in due time, but we may fail to obtain His blessing Matt. 22:1–14. This man made a great supper and bade many but some did not come; however, the man's house was filled with guests who accepted his invitation. One may fail to accept God's offer of mercy, but heaven will have plenty of people, for someone will judge himself unworthy of everlasting life Acts 13:46. The songwriter said:

> *Just as I am, without one plea;*
> *But that Thy blood was shed for me,*
> *And that Thou bidst me come to Thee,*
> *O Lamb of God I come, I come.*
> *Just as I am, and waiting not;*
> *To rid my soul of one dark blot;*
> *To Thee whose blood can cleanse each spot;*
> *O lamb of God I come, I come.*

> *Redemption Song Book #292*
> *Harper Collins Publishers,*
> *77-85 Fulham Palace Road, London, W6-8JB*

Notes:

37 – Reactions to the Gospel

Acts 17:22–34

The Apostle Paul and Barnabas were in the church at Antioch, they were called by God and commended from that assembly to minister up in Antioch in Pisidia and so forth, and then from Antioch in Syria to Antioch in Asia. Reaching Athens we see:

1. The ignorance in their object for worship at Athens Acts 17:22–23. Paul saw the city wholly given to idolatry, including a name they called the unknown God, so his spirit was stirred within him, and he presented Jesus Christ to them.

2. The introduction of the one to be worshipped Acts 17 vs. 24–26. God made the world and all things therein; seeing that he is Lord of heaven and earth, dwelleth not in temples made with hands. Paul gave them information on our ancestors from Adam—God made all men of one blood to dwell upon the face of the earth, and God is not worshipped with the works of men's hands, so they should seek the Lord.

3. The inclusion of all men to repent and the intention of God to judge the world Acts 17 vs. 30–31. God commanded all men to repent, which is a change of mind and attitude toward God by hating of sin.

4. Immediate response of the people Acts 17 vs. 32–34. Some mocked, some procrastinated, but some cleaved. They believed the gospel.

Notes:

38 – Resources in Crises
Exodus chapter 15-chapter 17:1-16

The journey of Israel from Egypt to Canaan is like a roller coaster, sometimes up and sometimes down. This reflects the lives of many Christians. They had now been victorious in crossing the Red Sea unto the Wilderness of Shur, but after three days they found no water. Then they came to Marah where there was water Exodus 15: 23, but they could not drink because the water was bitter, and there the people murmured against Moses. He cried unto the Lord who showed him a tree, which when he had cast into the water, the water was made sweet.

Leaving Marah they came to Elim, Exodus 15: 27 where were twelve wells of water and seventy palm trees, and they encamped there by the water. This is from adversity to tranquility, and sometimes we have such experiences. When I read this today, it brought memories to me about days when I was a young Christian and started preaching. I would go to very quiet places to meditate on my messages; in the country it may be among some trees, or in the city it may be in a graveyard. I remember a Sunday morning when a missionary gave a message on this:

"And they came to Elim where were twelve wells of water and seventy palm trees and they encamped there by the waters. Exodus 15: 27. That evening I went to a quiet place to meditate, and that place had many palm trees, each about twenty feet tall and a river, and there that message came to me, so I said let me count the palm trees, and when I counted them, there were seventy palm trees. The Bible came alive, and that was in Grenada in the Caribbean.

On another occasion; I was traveling from St. Thomas, a US Virgin Island, to Tortola, a British Virgin Island. Between these islands there are many small islands, some uninhabited. One day while traveling on a boat from St. Thomas to Tortola, I noticed one small island was very dry; no one lives there but only bushes. At that time I was mediating on the Day of Atonement in Leviticus 16:1-34.

Aaron shall take two goats and present them before the Lord at the door of the tabernacle, 16:1-34.and Aaron shall cast lots upon the two goats, one lot for the Lord and the other for the scapegoat, Aaron shall confess over the scapegoat the sins of the children of Israel, and this scapegoat shall be sent away by the hand of a fit man into the wilderness unto a land not inhabited and to be let go there.

When I saw the dry, uninhabited island, I said, "This island looks like the place where the scapegoat would have gone," and as soon as I said so, one lone goat raised up its head from the bushes. The Bible came alive again.

From one crisis to another, and so there is one victory to another. Leaving Elim they came to Rephidim where they had an experience of a war with Amalek vs. 8–16. Moses, Aaron and Hur went up to the top of the hill; when Moses held up his hand, Israel prevailed, and when Moses let down his hand, Amalek prevailed. Moses hands were heavy, so Joshua and Hur held up his hand (fellowship among brethren for victory is necessary) and then Israel prevailed. Amalek was defeated. The songwriter said:

> What various hindrances we meet;
> In coming to the Mercy Seat!
> Yet who, that knows the worth of prayer;
> But wishes to be often there.
> While Moses stood with arms spread wide,
> Success was found on Israel's side,
> But when through weariness they failed,
> That moment Amalek prevailed..

Redemption Song Book #600
Harper Collins Publishers,
77-85 Fulham Palace Road, London W6-8JB

Notes:

39 – Salvation by Looking Up

Isaiah 45:1–6, 22; Numbers 21

*I*srael was reminded that safety and salvation were to be found only in Jehovah. The experiences of Israel can be seen from their deliverance from bondage in Egypt to the wilderness, to the conquest of two kings on East Side Jordan, to the destruction of seven nations, and the possession of the Promised Land under the leadership of Moses and Joshua.

Salvation is by looking to God, who was manifest in the flesh in the person of Jesus Christ Phil. 2:1–6.When I was in public school, there was a lesson in the textbook with the title, *A Perilous Adventure*. The story was about some boys competing to carve their name the highest on a rock, and the one who can climb the highest to cave his name would be the hero. It so happened that one boy climbed the highest, but when he finished, he could not come down. The other boys got worried, so one of them went and called the parents of the boy who was stuck and couldn't come down. With this, many neighbors rushed to the scene, so there was a large crowd below. The father of the boy called to him, "William, William don't look down; keep your eyes toward heaven." The story goes on; the boy did not look down, and his eyes are fixed toward heaven.

Then one Good Samaritan went above the rock, threw a rope to the boy, and pulled him over the rock. While the boy was dangling over the crowd, the people groaned as they watched the boy above them. But, praise God, the boy was saved by looking up.

In Numbers 21:5–9, we read the children of Israel spake against God and against Moses.

And the Lord sent fiery serpents among the people, and they bit the people and much people died. The people came to Moses and said, we have sinned, for we have spoken against the Lord, and against thee. Then the Lord said unto Moses, make thee a serpent of brass, and set it upon a pole: and it shall come to pass that every one that is bitten, when he looketh upon it shall live.

Their salvation was only by looking up.

In the New Testament, in John 3:14–16 Jesus said:

And as Moses lifted up the serpent in the wilderness, even so must the son of man be lifted up, that whosoever believeth in him should not perish, but have eternal life. For God so loved the world, that he gave his only begotten Son, that whosoever believeth in him should not perish, but have everlasting life.

In Luke 13:22–23, there is a question: "Are there few that be saved?" (There is the urgency for salvation 2 Cor. 6:2).

Read Mark 10:17–26. Who then can be saved? (The dependency for salvation) The man in this passage was looking for a source other than Jesus.

In Jeremiah 8:20 we read, "The harvest is past, the summer is ended and we are not saved" (The complacency against salvation).

But in Jeremiah 8:22, the question is asked, Is there a balm in Gilead, is there no physician there? With reference to Christ, yes, there is a balm in Gilead, which is Christ himself. The songwriter wrote:

> *I've a message from the Lord, hallelujah!*
> *This message unto you I'll give,*
> *'Tis recorded in His word, hallelujah,*
> *It is only that you look and live.*
> *Chorus.*
> *"Look and live," my brother, live*
> *.... Look to Jesus now and live;*
> *'Tis recorded in His word; hallelujah,*
> *It is only that you look and live.*

Redemption Song Book #98
Harper Collins Publishers,
77-85 Fulham Palace Road, London W6-8JB

Notes:

40 – Separated! How to Return

Gen. 27:1–10; 28:1–5; 32:1—11 20; 33:1–11

*I*f there be a separation, there must first be a togetherness.

In Genesis 18:19, God said this of Abraham. "For I know him, that he will command his children and his household after him, and they shall keep; the way of the Lord to do justice and judgment." This implies that Jacob the grandson of Abraham came from a good family, and it is generally noticed that such children have good relationship and fellowship as they are growing up. (I can testify to this, coming from a family of ten children.) As we make this observation on the life of Jacob, we see a break in that relationship by the action of Jacob: (1) Jacob stole the birthright of his brother Esau, Gen. 25:34; and (2) Jacob stole the blessing from his brother Esau Gen. 27:26–29. Now therefore we can see:

1. The transgression of Jacob against his brother Esau, leading to a separation of the two Gen. 27:1–19. Jacob had to leave the house.

2. The separation of Jacob from Esau, leading to a break in a fellowship with his brother and parents. Jacob could not talk with them of the good old days. But two good things Jacob had going for him were that he had an uncle Laban at Haran he could go to, and God assured him that he, God, would bring him back to the land that he left Gen. 28. 10–21.

3. The intention of Jacob to be reconciled with his brother for restoration of fellowship Gen 32:1–20. First, plan no. 1: To give good news as to how the Lord had blessed him Gen.32:3–5. Prov. 25:25 says, As cold waters to a thirsty soul, so is good news from a far country, but he realized that would not work, for the messengers returned saying we came to thy brother Esau, and also he cometh to meet thee and four hundred men with him. This made Jacob afraid; conscience and good memory is very powerful.

Plan no 2 was to send a large present to Esau by the hand of his servants, yet Jacob was not assured of his acceptance, for he said, peradventure he will accept me Gen. 32:12–21. Even then that would not work for reconciliation, for the principle for reconciliation is by the acknowledgment of guilt Deut. 16:19. Jacob had to do just that, even after he divided his family by groups putting his beloved Rachael last, that in case Esau would smite the first two group, Rachael would survive. That would not work, either.

4. The confession of Jacob Gen. 33:1–3. Finally Jacob had to come and bow before Esau, acknowledging his guilt; he was then accepted by Esau (ref: The Prodigal Son Luke 15;18.

Again, all these present to us man's transgression before a Holy God Rom 5:12. Man's various attempts to be reconciled to God may include education or a high position in a company. Once at the end of a Gospel crusade, as a personal worker, I saw a man who was a big man in a company. I thought he was under conviction, so I went and attempted to talk to him about making a decision for Christ. He just laughed at me. Sometimes some people believe that by giving to charity or just going to church or good works will give them a place in heaven, but it's not so with a holy God. We must acknowledge we are sinners, confess our dependence on Christ for salvation, and accept him as our savior. This will bring about reconciliation, make us Christians and a candidate for heaven. The chorus says:

> There's a way back to God! from the dark parts of sin.
> There's a door that is open and we must go in.
> From Calvary's cross is where we begin,
> when we come as a sinner to Jesus.

Notes:

41 – Saved, Sanctified, and Called

Jude 1–25

The book of Jude was written about AD 66 and contains only twenty-five verses but is filled with divine truths of the past, present, and future. Whereas the theme of the book is contending for the faith once delivered unto the saints, meaning the apostles' doctrines, it also presents to us warnings against apostasy vs. 4–13 and unfulfilled prophecies, which are going to be fulfilled after the rapture of the church verse 14.

The writer is introduced as Jude, the brother of James and servant of Jesus Christ. Tracing the genealogy of Jude in Matt. 13:53–55, Mark 6:1–3, and Luke 6:16, we find him like James to be the half-brother of Jesus according to the flesh. At first the half-brothers of Jesus did not believe in him for they said in John 7:4–5, "If thou doest these things (that is, the miracles Jesus was doing), go shew yourself unto the world." We read, neither did his brethren believe in him, but comparing scriptures that after the death of Christ they believed ref: Acts 1:14. These all continued with one accord in prayer and supplication, with the women, and Mary the mother of Jesus and with his brethren, so they were charter members of the church when it began on the Day of Pentecost. Not only we have James as one of the elders in the church at Jerusalem, but Jude is also now writing his epistle.

Again Jude is introduced as a servant of Jesus. A servant does not do his own thing or follow the dictates of his own conscience but follows instructions from his master, so now Jude is following instructions of his master Jesus Christ. To whom is he writing? To them that are sanctified by God the father, preserved in Jesus Christ, and called. Who are they that were sanctified? How were they sanctified, and when were they sanctified? All this were done at the time of salvation, and we cannot explain the process of our salvation according to 1 Peter 1:2, John 3:8, and in John

9:25. The blind man said one thing I know that whereas I was blind now I see. And there is a song which says, "But it's real, its real I know it's real, praise God, for I know I know it's real." We are sanctified or set apart for God and preserved in Jesus Christ. One of the key verses to this is found in John 10:27–28, Romans 8:35–39, and 1 Peter 1:4–5. We cannot say, hold on my friend that you might make it to heaven, but we can say walk in the Spirit and you shall not fulfill the lust of the flesh, for the question is who is holding who. Suppose you are crossing the street with a four-year-old and holding his hand. If the child see something attractive to him on the road, but a car is coming, you will pull the child to safety, that the child be saved is a matter of who is holding who. So, praise God, we are not keeping ourselves, but we are being kept by God.

To them that are sanctified by God, Preserved in Jesus Christ, and called. What type of calling do we have? We have a holy calling 2 Tim 1:9 or a call unto a life of holiness that reflects the life of Christ.

We have a high calling. Phil 3:13–14 says:

Brethren, I count not myself to have apprehended; but this one thing I do, forgetting those things which are behind, and reaching forth unto those things which are before, I press toward the mark for the prize of the high calling of God in Christ Jesus.

This tells me that our service is not something of little importance! To think that God has made us His representatives that a person can go to heaven instead of going to hell, we should take our calling as very important, the highest job in the world.

We have a heavenly calling Heb. 3:1, that is, knowing our destination and living in view of that destination. Phil. 3:20 says, "Our conversation or citizenship is in heaven from whence we look for the Savior, our Lord Jesus Christ." We are pilgrims to a destination. The songwriter says:

> In the good old way where the saints have gone,
> And the King leads on before us,
> We are traveling home to the heavenly hills,

With the day-star shining o'er us.
Chorus:
Travelling home to the mansions fair,
Crowns of rejoicing and life to wear;
O what a shout when we all get there,
Safe in the glory land!

Redemption Song Book #422
Harper Collins Publishers
77-85 Fulham Palace Road, London W6-8JB

Notes:

42 – Sermon for a Thankful Heart
Psalms 68:19; Psalms 116:12

Blessed be the Lord who daily loadeth us with benefits. Psalms 68:19.

What shall I render unto the Lord for all His benefits toward me? Psalm 116:12

These are Psalms from David, and to fully understand and apply them to our daily lives, it is necessary to look at the life of David.

In 1 Samuel 21, David is seen going to the land of Nob unto Ahimelech the priest, who gave David and his 600 men the hallowed bread, which was not lawful for the common people, but for the priests, Ahimelech the priest also gave David the sword of Goliath, but there was a man there name Doeg of the house of Saul who went and told Saul that David visited the priest and was given the sword of Goliath. This led to Saul and Doeg to killing eighty-five priests, including Ahimelech, but Abiathar the son of Ahimelech escaped with one of the Ephod, that which the priests would wear, and he joined himself to David and his 600 men. David having left Nob had many trying experiences as King Saul pursued after him, but God delivered him out of them all.

In 1 Samuel 27:1, David said, "I shall now perish one day by the hand of Saul, I should speedily escape into the land of the Philistines. Therefore he went unto Achish the king of Gath who gave him a little inland town called Ziklag. It was not long after that war broke out between Israel and the Philistines, so at that time David was in enemy's territory, and he was prepared to go with the Philistines to fight against Israel. The advisors to the king suggested he should not go with them for fear he might be reconciled with his master Saul and turn against them for there was such a fame of his power 1 Sam. 29:5. They sent back David to his little inland town. The battle was fierce, and Saul died in Mount Gilboa. Following the death of Saul, David became king, first to Judah and then to all Israel.

Now, therefore, as David took a backward look at his life with respect to how the Lord saved, protected, sustained, and supplied his many needs, he could write Psalm 68:19 Blessed be the Lord who daily loadeth us with benefits. And then with a grateful heart he can ask himself this question: What shall I render unto the Lord for all His benefits toward me Psalm 116:12? David also wrote in Psalm 37:25, I have been young and now I am old I have never seen the righteous forsaken nor his seed begging bread.

By way of divine providence, we can see the benefit to David goes back far in history, and we can see how by God's grace we have been affected, with a continuous effect on our lives. To trace his genealogy, we see Ruth the Moabite coming with Naomi from the land of Moab where they worship Idols (see the book of Ruth chapters 1–4). Ruth married to Boaz, a kinsman/redeemer to the husband of Naomi. They had a son Obed, Obed had a son Jessie, and Jessie was the father of David to the genealogy of Jesus according to the flesh Luke 3:23–32.

As we make the application on the life of David to us who believe in God and His sovereign grace in the person of our Lord Jesus Christ, we too can shout Blessed be the Lord who daily loadeth us with benefits Psalm 68:19.What are the benefits we received from the Lord? (1) The benefit of His love 1 John 3:1. What kind of love God hath bestowed on us? His love is universal, John 3:16; his love is everlasting, Jeremiah 31:3; his love is freely given Hosea 14:4; his love is great John 4:13; and the benefit of communion and fellowship according to his promise to be with us Heb. 13:5.

Notes:

43 – Sermon on Worship

John 9:35–38, Luke 18:41–43; John 4:21–24

1. What is the definiti/on of worship? The expression of a grateful heart to the Lord for the greatest thing He has done for us as referenced in the above texts.

2. What is the motivation or the driving force for worship? In the cases of the blind men referred to in these passages, they considered their past condition, their sickness, their helplessness, and then their happiness because of what the Lord had done for them, bringing them to a place of joyfulness. In the case of the woman at the well, the object for her worship was the mountain at Jerusalem. Possibly she was knowledgeable of Psalm 121:1: I will lift up mine eyes unto the hills from whence cometh my help, my help cometh from the Lord. That was good for the days of David, but now a new day is about to unfold, that the true worshippers must worship the Father in spirit and in truth—not physical anymore but spiritual. So now we worship because of what Jesus has done for us Eph. 2:1–13; Col. 1:12–14.

3. When do we worship? In reference to our relationship, every time we remember where we were and now where we are before God, we should give thanks, singing or meditating on a song relating to our relationship with God.

    The story is told of a boy who lived in the country. He had no proper clothes, he had no shoes, and he did not have his own room, but one day a rich man from town came to the country. He got this boy from his parents and took him home with him in the city. The rich man took the boy to the store, bought him a blue suit of clothes and a pair of shoes, and gave him his own room at his house. The boy changed clothes, put his old clothes in the shoebox and was wearing his new clothes, but every time he would go to his room, he would come out laughing. One day the rich man followed him to his room and noticed he was looking into the shoebox where he put his old clothes. The rich man said to him, "Why are you keeping these old clothes?" The boy said, "Every time I look at these old clothes and see how I am today, I get happy, and I am thankful to you for making me who I am and what I have today." This is an illustration for worship.

4. What worship is not: it is not a time of confession. David confessed his sins in Psalm 51.

    It is not a time of supplication or begging; see the prayer of Jabez in 1 Chron 4:9–10. It is not a time of intercession or pleading with God on behalf of others 1 Tim 2:1–4. It is not a time of exhortation Acts 20:28–30. These are parts for the prayer and ministry meetings. But it is a time of reflection on the grace of God and the death, burial, resurrection, and ascension of Christ.

Notes:

44 – Soldiers of Christ Arise

2 Timothy 2:1–10

To all who have received Christ as Savior, have entered into a relationship with him, have an identity in him, are expected to take a stand for him, and continue in that stand for the remainder of his or her life here, or unto the coming of Christ for His own, in consideration to this, we find that those of us who have taken this most important step in life are now identified with Christ and have been given a name in the scripture as believers Acts 5:14, brethren John 1–12, Christians Acts 11:26, saints Romans. 1:7, and soldiers 2 Timothy 2:3.

The requirements of a soldier are (a) know your enemy, Eph. 6:12; (2) know your weapon, 2 Cor. 10:4; and (3) be ready for warfare, Romans 1:15; and (4) be obedient to orders as given by superiors, 2 Timothy 4:1–2. Therefore, to be a soldier of Christ there must be:

1. The personal acceptance and genuine faith in Christ Romans 10:9–10.
2. The preparation for service and total submission to Christ Romans 1:16 by prayer, reading his word, fellowship with Christ and members of His church, putting on the whole armor of Christ as recorded in Ephesians 6:10–18, showing ourselves approved unto God and rightly dividing the word of truth 2 Timothy 2:15. AWANA stands for Approved Workmen Are Not Ashamed (ref: Philip the evangelist was quite ready when he met the Ethiopian eunuch Acts 8:35; he began in the same scripture Isaiah 53:7).
3. The pursuit to the objective and steadfastness in our service for Christ 2 Tim. 2:3, 11; 4:6–8.
4. The pleasure to be revealed and the satisfaction to be realized (Eph. 5:27 and 2 Thess 2:1) at the second coming of Christ.

Finally, in view of these, let us arise, dedicate and consecrate ourselves unto God for the fulfillment of His will in us.The songwriter wrote:

> *Stand up! stand up for Jesus! Ye soldiers of the cross;*
> *Lift high His royal banner, It must not suffer loss.*
> *From victory, unto victory His army shall He lead,*
> *Till every foe is vanquished, And Christ is Lord indeed.*
> *Chorus*
> *Stand up, stand up for Jesus, Ye soldiers of the cross,*
> *Lift high His royal banner, It must not suffer loss.*
>
> *Redemption Song Book #52*
> *Harper Collins Publishers,*
> *77-85 Fulham Place Road, London W6-8JB*

Notes:

45 – Spiritual Motivation for Evangelism

Ezekiel 22:30, Isa. 6:1–6, 1 Sam. 30:1–10, 18–25

*A*nd I sought for a man from among them, that should make up the hedge, and stand in the gap before me for the land, that I should not destroy it, but I found none Ezekiel 22:30.

1. The occasion of this verse was due to the situation in Israel as we can see from verses Ezekiel 22 vs 16–29. Israel was indicted for their disobedience vs. 6–16, and they were advised of judgments that would come vs. 17–22. The priests, princes, prophets, and the people were told that their practices were not helping the conditions they were in. Therefore, God was looking for a man to stand for Him Ezekiel 22:vs. 30. What must be the qualification of that man? He must be one who knows their language, customs, and practices; he must be one who is prepared in heart for that mission; he must be one who has a burden for their salvation; he must be one who is knowledgeable of God's word and God's judgment; and he must be one who is ready to stand at the gap, one whose objectives are to bring glory to God, and also one who believes that God is able to keep, protect, and sustain him.

2. The occupation is that on an individual basis. God is calling for you Isaiah 6:1–6. In the year that King Uzziah died I saw also the Lord siting upon the throne, high and lifted up, and his train filled the temple. It's a sad but interesting story on the death of Uzziah 2 Chron. 26:1–23. He was prosperous while he served the Lord, but he did that which was not his calling even though he was warned by eighty-five priests of his action. However, he insisted to have his own way; he ended up with leprosy and died. In that year Isaiah got his calling from the Lord in that we read:

   In the year that king Uzziah died I saw also the Lord sitting upon a throne high and lifted up, and his train filled the temple. . . . Then said I, woe is me for I am undone, because I am a man of unclean lips, and I dwell in the midst of a people of unclean lips, for mine eyes have seen the King, the Lord of hosts. Then flew one of the seraphim unto me, having a live coal in his hand, which he had taken with the tongs from of the altar. And he laid it upon my mouth, and said, Lo, this hath touched thy lips, and thine iniquity is taken away and thy sin purged. . . . Also I heard the voice of the Lord saying, Whom shall I send and who will go for us? Then said I, Here am I, send me.

He did not say, "I know someone whom you can send, or I will think about it, or I don't think I am qualified because I have to take some theological training first before I can go, everyone to go may not have the financial resources to attend an accredited school before answering the call of God." In Matt. 28:19 Jesus said Go! Some of them were fishermen, and fishermen do not always have college degrees, so the call is to anyone who has the qualification mentioned above. Then the going is not always to foreign fields. Many of us began at our Jerusalem, at home, and as the Lord opens the way and the doors, we go.

The songwriter says:

> There's a call comes ringing o'er the restless wave,
> Send the light! Send the light!
> There are souls to rescue, there are souls to save,
> Send the light! Send the light!
> Chorus:
> Send the light, the blessed Gospel light!
> Let it shine from shore to shore.
> Send the light... and let its radiant beams,
> Light the world... for evermore.
>
> Redemption Song Book #628
> Harper Collins Publishers,
> 77—85 Fulham Palace Road, London W6-8JB

Notes:

46 – Stepping into the Unknown

Joshua 3:1–4

W e rejoice today as to how great the United States is, but it was not easy for the first thirteen colonies when they stepped out from Britain to be a nation, for there were many unforeseen issues and circumstances of which they had no knowledge of or what to expect.

In view of this we can see Israel leaving Egypt for the land of Canaan. We can consider:

1. The call of Moses to lead from Egypt to the land of Moab. What experiences they had at the Red Sea, including the bitter water at Marah, the worshiping of the calf at Sinai, the battle with Amalek, murmurings and complaining, and so on until Moses died at Mount Nebo in the land of Moab Deut. 34:5.

2. The call of Joshua to take over from Moses from Moab to Canaan. Moses my servant is dead, now therefore arise Joshua 1:1–5. However we see God's promise to Joshua: As I was with Moses so I will be with thee. Now we see the children of Israel about to leave the land of Moab for Canaan; the key words to them are—for ye have not passed this way heretofore Joshua 3:1–4.

3. The preparation to the unknown Chapter 3: vs 1. And Joshua arose early in the morning, and they moved from Shittim and came to Jordan, he and all the children of Israel, 600,000 men beside women and children and a mix multitude.

4. The instructions regarding the unknown chapter 3:1–17. And it came to pass after three days that the officers went through the host, and they commanded the people saying; "When ye see the Ark of the Covenant of the Lord your God, and the priest the Levites bearing it, then ye shall remove from our place, and go after it." But before they leave Moab to cross the Jordan River unto Gilgal, they must be prepared to follow instructions.

Application: We are journeying toward the unknown for the year 2017 with life's blessing and problems, but there is one who knows, even God the creator, upholder, and sustainer. Finally we are journeying unto eternity, for we pass this way but once; our destination is either heaven or hell. In heaven there is the promise of untold blessings. To those of us who have accepted Christ as our Savior, Jesus said in John 14:1–3; "Let not your heart be troubled, ye believe in God believe also in me. I go to prepare a place for you, and if I go I will come again to receive you unto myself, that where I am there ye may be also." To those who fail to accept Christ as Savior we read in Revelation 20:11; And I saw a great white throne, and him that sat on it, from whose face the earth and the heaven fled away, and there was found no place for them (them means people). Therefore it's important to heed God's word now cf Heb. 2:1.

In Numbers chapter 10:vs 29 we read, Moses said unto Hobab, the son of Raguel, the Midianite, Moses father-in law (that makes him Moses brother-in law); "We are journeying unto a place which the Lord said, I will give it you: come thou with us, and we will do thee good: for the Lord hath spoken good concerning Israel. But Hobab said unto him, I will not go. But I will depart to mine own land and to my kindred.

It was also Orpah who failed to go with Naomi and Ruth to Bethlehem-Judah and returned to her gods in the land of Moab Ruth 1:14–15.

We are journeying unto a place which the Lord said He will give to us, and that place we find in 1 Cor. 2:9–10 concerning those of us who put our trust in Christ. We say come thou with us, for the Lord hath spoken good concerning those who are saved.The songwriter said:

> Come every soul by sin oppress'd;
> There's mercy with the Lord.
> And He will surely give you rest;
> By trusting in His word.
> Chorus;
> Only trust Him, Only trust Him;

Only trust Him now.
He will save you, He will save you,
He will save you now.

Redemption Song Book # 196
Harper Collins Publishers,
77-85 Fulham Palace Road, London, W6-8JB

Notes:

47 – Strength and Hope from a Boy's Lunch

Luke 9:10–17; John 6:1–14

The information given in both books presents to us the boy, his lunch, and the impact that lunch had on the people who were following Jesus. In Luke 9:1–17, we see:

1. The sending of Jesus's twelve disciples to preach the kingdom of God with power and authority Luke 9 vs. 1–5
2. The surrendering to the instruction of Jesus by the disciples vs. 6, they departed and did what they were told to do. They preached the gospel of the kingdom
3. The shocking news to Herod was that the gospel was being preached by someone other than John the Baptist, so he said John have I beheaded. He remembered what happened when his daughter brought the head of John the Baptist in a plate before him and his friends after she danced, so he said John had been beheaded vs. 9.
4. The suggestion of the disciples when they saw there was nothing to eat, and they couldn't do anything about the situation was met by Jesus' response: send the multitude away vs. 12.
5. The scarcity of the food: only one boy had five loaves and two fishes, and there were over 5,000 people to be fed vs. 13–15.
6. The sufficiency with Christ. They all ate and took up twelve baskets full with what was left.

In John 6:1–14, we find the same story, for it seems that it was a small boy and his mother fixed his lunch for him, but we can take note about the action of the boy when he saw the need arise and what was required of him. He did not know that his action would have such an impact in the lives of 5,000 people, but we can see that when the boy was approached:

He responded immediately,

He responded voluntarily,

He responded unreservedly.

Now we can see the reliance on the boy; their lunch was dependent on the obedience of the boy. They all did eat and were satisfied. Their satisfaction was by the obedience and action of the boy.

Their continuance with the Lord was by the strength they received as a result of the action of the boy; he yielded his lunch that others might be strengthened.

There is always an application to this relevant to our walk with the Lord, and how we can be a blessing to others that they too may follow the Lord. It is called yieldedness to God that he may use us for the salvation of many and for those who are weary in their walk with the Lord, that they may be encouraged.

What do we have? Wisdom, talent, skills, money, and so forth. We pray that we may lay it down at the feet of Jesus, for this may bring satisfaction to others or strengthen them in the faith. Some may have come to our services for the first time and learn of following Jesus. We can think of the 5,000 people; many may have joined the crowd for the first time, so they did not return home the same way as they came.

Notes:

48 – Studies on the Life and Works of Deborah, the Woman
Judges, chapters 4–5

The children of Israel were led by Moses, the servant of God, from Egypt to the edge of the river of Jordan, and then by Joshua from Jordan to the conquest and possession of Canaan. After the death of Joshua, they were ruled by thirteen judges for about 450 years Acts 13:20, Deborah having been the fifth judge.

The characteristic of that age is found in the book of Judges: "Every man did that which was right in his own eyes." This ended in utter failure, as it generally is by leaning unto our own way Proverbs 3:5. With this we see:

1. The death of Joshua Judges 2:8. And Joshua the son of Nun, the servant of the Lord, died, being an hundred and ten years. And they buried him in the border of his inheritance in Timnath-Pheres, in the mount of Ephraim, on the North side of the hill Gaash.

2. The departure of Israel from God's way Judges 2:12. And they forsook the Lord God of their fathers, which brought them out of the land of Egypt, and followed other gods, of the gods of the people that were round about them, and bowed themselves unto them, and provoked the Lord to anger.

3. The distress of Israel by their disobedience Judges 2:14. And the anger of the Lord was hot against Israel, and He delivered them into the hands of spoilers that spoiled them, and he sold them into the hands of their enemies round about, so that they could not any longer stand before their enemies.

4. The deliverance of Israel by the judges, as Deborah, the fifth judge. Who was Deborah—a judge, a wife, a prophetess, a mother Judges 4:5

5. The prophecy of Deborah Judges 4:6–7. And she sent and called Barak, the son of Abinoam out of Kadesh-Naphtali, and said unto him. Hath not the Lord God of Israel command saying go and draw

toward mount Tabor, and take with the ten thousand men of the children of Naphtali, and of the children of Zebulun?

6. The partnership with Deborah Judges 4:8–9. And Barak said unto her, If thou wilt go with me, then I will go: but if thou wilt not go with me, then I will not go.

7. The plan of Sisera, captain to the king of Canaan Judges 4:13. And Sisera gathered together all his chariots, even nine hundred chariots of iron, and all the people that were with him, from Harosheth of the Gentiles unto the river of Kishon.

8. The presence of God for deliverance of Israel Judges 4:14–24. And Deborah said unto Barak; Up; for this is the day in which the Lord hath delivered Sisera into thine hand; is not the Lord gone out before thee?

9. The praise of Deborah Judges 5:1–3. Then sang Deborah and Barak (partners whom God used to deliver Israel) Praise ye the Lord for the avenging of Israel, when the people willingly offered themselves.

The application: when the Lord calls for a specific duty, we must be sensitive, obedient, and willing to work with whomever He has made available to us. One does not have to be great, for God can use anyone.

Look at some of the judges God used:

Othniel—Caleb's younger brother
Ehud—The left-handed judge with a dagger
Shamgar—Slew 600 Philistines with an ox goad
So God uses anyone who places his/her trust in him:
Men, Women, Boys, and Girls.

Notes:

49 – Studies from the Book of 1 Thessalonians 1–4

The book of 1 Thessalonians was written by the apostle Paul from Corinth in Greece AD 54. The message, which is relevant for our times, pertains to salvation, sanctification, and service in view of the soon coming again of Christ for His own.

The writing includes:

1. A word of salutation. The church of the Thessalonians which is in God the Father and the Lord Jesus Christ: grace and peace: grace comes before peace, for it is the grace of God that bringeth salvation Titus 2:11. And being justified by faith we have peace with God through our Lord Jesus Christ Rom. 5:1.

2. A word of commendation vs. 10: (a) their work of faith; They turn to God from Idols; (b) their labor of love to serve the living and true God; and (c) their patience of hope in our Lord Jesus Christ. Their waiting for His Son from heaven. In their labor they were also church planters, for they brought the message of salvation to Achaia. Many received the word so that in Acts 18; 24–28, we read of Apollos whom Aquila and Priscilla gave doctrinal instructions. He then went to Achaia and helped that little church in their ministries.

3. A word of explanation as to what may happen to a Christian as he faithfully serves the Lord 1st Peter4:12.

Notes:

50 – Studies from the Gospel of John

Travels, Teaching, and Testimony of Jesus

In chapter 5:33–39, Jesus gave a message on the fourfold witness of Himself: (1) the witness of Christ by John the Baptist; (2) the witness of Christ by His works; (3) the witness of Christ by the Father; and (4) the witness of Christ by the Scriptures.

In 6:67–71, Jesus asked His disciples whether they would go away from him, who is the ultimate for a meaningful life and an eternity of endless joy. Simon Peter said, "To whom shall we go, or there is none besides Thee, and no other source for consideration, Thou hast the words of eternal life.

Now in chapter 7 Jesus presented himself to all as the one who can meet our spiritual and physical needs, and also gave us an invitation to come unto him that such needs be met to overflowing. With these we can consider:

1. The timeliness of his movement John 7 vs. 1–10. Jesus walked in Galilee until the time for the Feast of Tabernacle at Jerusalem. There his brethren according to the flesh said to him; Depart hence, and go into Judaea, that thy disciples also may see the works that thou doest. For there is no man that doeth anything in secret, and he himself seeketh to be known openly. If Thou do these things, shew thyself to the world. For neither did his brethren believe in him. Jesus said unto them, My time is not yet come. (At least at that time His brethren did not believe in Him, but when we read Acts 1:14 we see the brethren of Jesus was in that upper room; they believed in him later). God's timing is not before the right time.

2. The teaching of God's doctrine John 7 vs. 14–36. Doctrine means the teaching of the truth in relation to God as he deals in his grace with all of the human race, that is, the doctrine of God that includes man, sin, Christ, the new birth, salvation, grace, faith, heaven, hell,

the ascension, and the return of Christ. The condition for knowing the doctrine of God is by doing His will Chapter 7 vs. 17.

3. The testimony of the Holy Spirit chapter 7 vs. 37–39. In the last day, that great day of the feast or the last of the seven feast days in Leviticus 23, Jesus stood and cried, saying, If any man thirst let him come unto me and drink. He that believeth on me, as the scripture hath said, out of his belly shall flow rivers of living water. But this spake he of the Spirit, which they that believe on him should receive; for the Holy Ghost was not yet given, because that Jesus was not yet glorified.

Notes:

CHAPTER 6

51 – Study to Show Thyself Approved unto God

2 Timothy 2:15–26

The apostle Paul, giving young Timothy an exhortation to be a good minister of God's word, said that we who minister the word must make sure we are approved by God, for a workman needeth not to be ashamed but rightly dividing the word of truth. I believe this is the text the AWANA clubs used as their motto:

"APPROVED WORKMEN ARE NOT ASHAMED"

1. The presentation of ourselves 2nd Timothy 2 vs. 15. God must be the object of our faith, the object of our love, the object of our life and ministry, and that in all things He might have the preeminence (the first place) Colossians. 1:18, cf Gal. 1:10, Eph. 6:6. Then we will be approved by Him, and thereby be used by Him. We may not have the approval of certain men or brethren, but once we have the approval of God, we can minister his word, and we should not be ashamed.

2. The proclamation of God's word 2nd Timothy 2 vs. 15b by rightly dividing the word of truth. There is a right way and a wrong way. To be assured of the right way, we must study the Bible, not as a storybook, but as God's communication with mankind and with the knowledge that it is relevant for all times. For the right way, read Nehemiah 8:5–6 and Ezra 8:10. For the wrong way—handling the word of God deceitfully—read 2 Cor. 4:2 and 2 Timothy 2:16–18.

3. The precaution against crafty deceptions 2nd Timothy 2 vs. 22–23. Flee youthful lust, and do not ask foolish and unlearned questions. All these are not profitable and will increase like termites. A little leaven leaveneth the whole lump. Nevertheless, the foundation of God standeth sure.

4. The pleasure of God in genuine Christians 2nd Timothy 2vs. 20–21. Christendom is a mixture of genuine Christians, professing Christians,

or those having a form of godliness but are not genuinely saved, and those clearly seen as non-Christians. By their fruits you shall know them. In Galatians 5:17–23, we have the evidences.

May we all be genuine Christians, approved by God and rightly dividing the word of truth, for the salvation of precious souls and the edification of the saints.

Notes:

52 – Studies on the Covenants

There are eight covenants of God dealing with the human race from the creation of man to the time in which we live: the covenant at Eden, with Adam, with Noah, with Abraham, with Moses, with the Palestinian, with David, and the New Covenant with us.

The Scripture relating to these covenants are: Eden—Gen. 1:28–30, 2:8–17; Adam—Gen. 3:15; Noah—Gen. 9:1; Abraham—Gen. 15:18; Moses—Exodus 20:3–17; Palestinian—Deut. 30:1–3; David—2 Samuel 7:16; and the New Covenant—Hebrews 8:7–13.

The definition of a covenant: An agreement, to promise by a covenant (Webster).

The immutability of the covenants is determined by who God is: "That by two immutable things, in which it was impossible for God to lie, we might have a strong consolation, who have fled for refuge to lay hold upon the hope set before us Heb. 6:18.

As we study the covenants and their meanings and fulfillments, there are two which stand out to us with reference to worship. They are the Mosaic and the New Covenant for in Hebrews 9, we read, "Then verily the first covenant had also ordinances of divine service, and a worldly sanctuary." This speaks of the approach to God for worship, which can be found in the book of Leviticus chapter 1: 1-17.

The approach to God was in the tabernacle, a physical structure, with a high priest from the tribe of Levi, and the approach to God through the great High Priest, our Lord Jesus Christ, without a physical structure, and we can come boldly with full assurance of acceptance Heb. 9:19.

In the Mosaic covenant, we see the high priest would be changed; and they truly were many priests because they were not suffered or (permitted) to continue by reason of death Hebrews. 7:23. In the New Covenant we read, but this man, Jesus Christ, because he continueth forever hath an unchangeable priesthood Hebrews.7:24. This is so encouraging.

The offering of the first covenant Leviticus chapter 1: 1–10 must be a male without blemish, a cattle, a sheep or goat, or two turtle doves, and the offerer must bring it of his own voluntary will and to be identified with it by putting his hand upon the head of the burnt offering. With this we see:

The method of approach: voluntary

The measure of appreciation: bringing a bullock, a lamb, a goat or two turtledoves.

The manner of appropriation: how he sees his need for atonement.

The offering of the new covenant: For if the blood of bulls and of goats, and the ashes of an heifer sprinkling the unclean, sanctifieth to the purifying of the flesh: How much more shall the blood of Christ, who through the eternal Spirit offered himself without spot to God Hebrews. 9:13–14. By His own blood he entered in once into the holy place, having obtained eternal redemption for us Heb. 9:12.

In the Mosaic covenant with the Levitical priesthood: on the Day of Atonement the requirement was an annual sacrifice by the high priest for himself and family and one for the people Lev. 16:1–34. With the high priestly work of Christ we read, but in those sacrifices there is a remembrance again made of sins every year, for it is not possible that the blood of bulls and of goats should take away sins Heb. 10:3–4.

In the new covenant we read Hebrews 10:vs 12, But this man, Jesus Christ, after he had offered one sacrifice for sins for ever sat down on the right hand of God. Then in chapter 9, vs. 12, we read; And by His own blood he entered in once into the holy place, having obtained eternal redemption for us. Notice the word *obtained* in the past tense, meaning completed.

However, the first covenant had a glorious administration 2 Cor. 3:7. At least every year on the Day of Atonement, the Israelites could go home with a sense of relief. The New Covenant has a ministration which exceeds in glory 2 Cor. 3:8. We can come to God any time and at any place. *Songwriter says;*

Done is the work that saves,
Once and forever done;
Finished the righteousness That clothes the unrighteous one,
The love that blesses us below,
Is flowing freely to us now.

The sacrifice is o'er;
The veil is rent in twain,
The mercy seat is red;
With blood of victim slain,
Why stand we then without in fear?
The blood of Christ invites us near.

The Believers Hymn Book #45
Horatius Bonar, Sold at John Ritchie LTD,
Kilmarnock, Scotland

Notes:

53 – Studies on the Dispensations from Eternity to Eternity

Whereas some Bible scholars may have a different breakdown on the dispensations, I would like to use the breakdown by C. I. Scofield.

First of all, let us have the definition on a dispensation. A dispensation is a period of time during which man is tested in respect of obedience to some specific revelation of the will of God.

The first dispensation is known as the dispensation of *innocency* Gen. 1:27—2:16. In Genesis 1:26, we read; And God said Let us make man in our image after our likeness, and in Gen 1:27, we read, So God created man in his own image. In chapter 1:26 the pronouns are plural, but in chapter 1:27 they are singular. In Deuteronomy 6:4 we read, Hear O Israel, the Lord our God is one God. In Ecclesiastes 7:29 we read, God created man upright or perfect. In Genesis 2:15 we read, And the Lord God took the man and put him into the Garden of Eden to dress it and to keep it. Therefore man was put in the garden in innocence.

The second dispensation is known as the dispensation of *conscience* Gen 2:16; 8:20. In Genesis 2:16 we read, And the Lord God commanded the man saying, Of every tree of the garden thou mayest freely eat. But of the tree of the knowledge of good and evil, thou shall not eat of it, for in the day that thou eatest thereof thou shall surely die. In Genesis chapter 3:1–7, Adam and Eve were deceived by the devil, disobeyed God, and brought down all the generation that would be born to be sinners before a holy God Romans 5:12. Adam and Eve became conscious of their sins and sewed fig leaves to cover themselves from the presence of the Lord. God drove them out of the garden Genesis. 3: vs 24.

In Genesis chapter 6 we read, when men began to multiply on the face of the earth and daughters were born unto them; that the sons of God saw the daughters of men that they were fair, and they took them wives of all which they chose. It has been taught that this mean the sons of God there are from the descendants of Seth, righteous ones, and daughters of men are from the descendants of Cain, the unrighteous one, being then mixed marriages.

And God said My Spirit shall not always strive with man, for that he also is flesh, yet his days shall be an hundred and twenty years. But Noah found grace in the eyes of the Lord, God gave Noah instructions to build an ark, Noah did so while he was preaching to the people, Noah a preacher of righteousness 2 Peter 2:5. God never brings His judgments before He brings His warnings. This case was the judgment of the flood that brought the end of the second dispensation Gen. 8:20.

The third dispensation is known as the dispensation of *human government* Gen. 8:20—12:3. In Genesis 8:20 we read when Noah came from the Ark after the water of the flood took 150 days to dry up, he built an altar unto the Lord and took of every clean beast, and of every clean fowl, and offered burnt-offerings on the altar. In Genesis 9:6, God gave Noah instructions for human government; Whoso sheddeth man's blood, by man shall his blood be shed, for in the image of God made he man.

The fourth dispensation known as the dispensation of *promise* Gen. 12:1–3 to Exodus 19:8. In Genesis 12:1–3 we read; now the Lord had said unto Abram whose name was later changed to Abraham, Get thee out of thy country, and from thy kindred, and from thy father's house, unto a land that I will shew thee. And I will make of thee a great nation, and I will bless thee, and make thy name great, and thou shalt be a blessing. And I will bless them that bless thee and curse them that curseth thee, and in thee shall all the families of the earth be blessed. This means that one will come from his line or he will be a Jew according to the flesh cf. John 4:9.

The fifth dispensation known as the dispensation of the *law* Exodus 19:8; Matt. 27:51. Moses had now returned from the mount and spoke to the people what God had commanded him. And all the people answered together, and said, All that the Lord hath spoken we will do. And Moses returned the words of the people unto the Lord. God gave 603 laws plus the Ten Commandments. Thus the dispensation of the Law was given and ended when Jesus died on the cross Matt. 27:51. The veil of the temple was rent in two.

The sixth dispensation known as the dispensation of *grace*, from Matt. 27:51 to an indefinite period of time unto the rapture of the church 1 Thess. 4:13–18. I have calculated that so far we are in the 1984th year of grace. How did I arrive at that figure? If Jesus was thirty-three years when he died, and we are now in 2017, and if grace began at the death of Jesus, then it is 2017 − 33 = 1984 and counting. For the law was given by Moses, but grace and truth came by Jesus Christ John 1:17. Christ is the end of the Law Romans 10:4.

Finally, the seventh dispensation, unlike the others, is known as the dispensation of the kingdom age or the dispensation of the *fullness of time* Ephesians 1:10. When would this be and how?

After the rapture of the church, there will be the seven years of tribulation and the manifestation of the Antichrist, the last world leader for Gentile World Empire, from Nebuchadnezzar to the Antichrist 2 Thess. 2:1–12. Then Christ will return, known as the revelation of Christ, to set up His earthly kingdom when He will reign as King of kings and Lord of lords. In Isaiah 9:7 we read, of the increase of his government and peace there shall be no end. Who will be with him? In 2 Thess. 2:1 we read, now we beseech you brethren by the coming of our Lord Jesus Christ, and by our gathering together unto him. And Revelation 5:10 says we shall reign on the earth.

If you are not a believer, a Christian, you will not be reigning with Christ, and if Christ comes for the believers before you die and left you behind you, will be one for the Antichrist. It's frightening to think of the experiences; therefore, the word today is still to believe on the Lord Jesus Christ and thou shall be saved from the horrible experiences with the Antichrist and hell forever Acts 16:31.

After the seven years of tribulation and Christ begins to rule, there will be the 1,000-year reign of Christ on this earth and then to be with him for all eternity. But it all starts now. Behold now is the accepted time, behold now is the day of salvation 2 Cor. 6:2. The songwriter said:

Where will you spend eternity?
This question comes to you and me!
Tell me , what shall your answer be!
Where will you spend eternity?
Chorus.
Eternity, Eternity! Where wilt thou spend eternity?

Redempton Son Book #260
Harper Collins Publishers, 77-85
Fulham Palace Road, London, W6-8JB

Notes:

54 – Studies from the Book of Hebrews, Chapter 1

The writer of the book of Hebrews is unknown, but it is assumed it was the apostle Paul according to 2 Peter 3:15, where Peter, who wrote to scattered Jews, said, even as our Bro. Paul had written unto you.

Hebrews chapter 1 presents the greatness of our salvation by the greatness of Christ. There we see:

The greatness of Christ by communication Hebrews 1 vs.1–2. God, who at sundry times and in divers manners spake in time past unto the fathers by the prophets, hath in these last days spoken unto us by his son, whom he hath appointed heir of all things, by whom also he made the worlds;

Whereas in times past God would speak to individuals and nations through the major and minor prophets, which was great; He has now spoken to us by Jesus Christ, one greater then Jonah Matt. 12:41.

The greatness of Christ by attraction; Hebrews 1 vs. 3. Who being the brightness of his glory, and the express image of his person; multitudes were attracted by His words and works. "And it came to pass when Jesus had ended these sayings, (the beatitudes) the people were astonished at his doctrine. For he taught them as one having authority, and not as the scribes Matt. 7:28–29.

The greatness of Christ by extraction. Who by Himself purged our sins vs. 3. Purging speaks of taking out, and that is what He does as we receive Him as our Savior. He takes away our sins; behold the Lamb of God who taketh away the sin of the world John 1:29.

The greatness of Christ by his preeminence. Better than the angels Hebrews 1 vs. 4–7, 13–14. That in all things He must have the preeminence (the first place) Colossians 1:1, 8

The greatness of Christ by His Deity Hebrews 1 vs.8. But unto the Son he saith, Thy throne O God is forever and ever a sceptre of righteousness is the sceptre of thy kingdom.

The greatness of Christ by His personal uprightness and personal excellence Hebrews 1 vs. 9. Thou hast loved righteousness, and hated iniquity, therefore God, even thy God, hath anointed thee with the oil of gladness above thy fellows.

The greatness of Christ by His pre-incarnation and unchangeableness Hebrews 1 vs. 10–14 And Thou Lord, in the beginning had laid the foundation of the earth; and the heavens are the works of thine hands cf. Psalm 102:26–27.

Notes:

55 – Studies from the Book of Hebrews, Chapter 2

This chapter begins by telling us we ought to give heed, pay attention to the things we have heard, whether from the prophets, angels, or from God's servants who speak God's word, for God will hold us responsible for what we have heard Hebrews 2 Hvs. 1–4.

The Greatness and Authority of Christ

The Greatness and Authority of Christ. Unto the Angels hath He not put in subjection, the world to come. There are three worlds mentioned in the scriptures; the world that then was being overflowed with water that is the world in Noah's day, the world that now is, in our time, and the world to come, when there will be a new heaven and a new earth. Nevertheless we, according to his promise look for new heavens and a new earth, wherein dwelleth righteousness 2 Peter 3:13.

The Humiliation and Exaltation of Christ

But we see Jesus who was made a little lower than the Angels for the suffering of death, crowned with glory and honor vs. 9. Forasmuch then as the children are partakers of flesh and blood, he also himself likewise took part of the same, that through death he might destroy him that had the power of death that is the devil. And deliver them who through fear of death were all their lifetime subject to bondage vs. 14–15; cf. Phil. 2:6–8.

Notes:

56 – Studies from the Book of Hebrews, Chapter 3

*I*n Hebrews chapter 3:7–19, we see the generation that came out of Egypt and their journey to the land of Canaan. We see the failure of many, which prevented them from reaching the Promised Land. Whereas we see the failure of many which prevented them from reaching the Promised Land, we can find an application, which relates to us as believers, who may be hindered from enjoying the rest the Lord Jesus spoke of in Matthew 11:28.

In verse 7 we read, wherefore as the Holy Ghost saint: Today if ye will hear his voice. In how many ways does the Lord speaks to mankind? We can see four ways. The Lord spoke by the God-head Deut. 6:4, by his Son Heb.1:1, by the Holy Spirit Heb. 3:7, and by the prophets Heb. 1:1. When must we hear him? Today or whenever He speaks to us. What was the response by those who heard Him? See vs. 9. How did God felt by their action? God grieved Hebrews 3 vs. 10; what was God's plan for those who grieved Him? See vs. 11. What is the exhortation for us by their action? See vs. 12–13; cf. Romans 15:4; 1 Cor. 10:1–6.

For we are made partakers of Christ, if we hold the beginning of our confidence steadfast unto the end vs. 14. This verse is the same as in vs.6. These verses do not suggest we need to hold on to be saved. The letter was sent to save Jews. For we read in Ephesians. 2:8–9, for by grace are we saved, and also in Titus 3:5. But rather, as in Heb. 10:23; Let us hold fast our profession or confidence of our salvation. This also means true discipleship cf. John 8:30–31.

For some, when they had heard did provoke, howbeit not all that came out of Egypt by Moses Jude 1:5. When was Israel saved? Was it from Egypt, or was it by the application of the blood on the doorpost? Was it when they reached the Promised Land? Hebrews. 3:16. It was by the application of the blood; Canaan was the place for their enjoyment, a land flowing with milk and honey according to God's covenant with Abraham Genesis 13:14–18.

In Matt. 11:28 Jesus said, Come unto me and I will give you rest. As we come and accept Him as our Savior, he gives us rest. But many in Israel did not enter their rest at Canaan due to provocation or sin against the Lord, for example, see Numbers 13:26–33. We can deny ourselves of the enjoyment of the rest that is in Christ Jesus. As their problem came due to sin, so the believer can fail to enjoy the peace and fellowship with the Lord because of sin, and God can bring also judgment to the believer. See 1 Cor. 15:28–32.

However, Canaan is not a type of heaven because there was fighting there. We can be liken as being in the wilderness in our pilgrimage unto heaven. In Eph. 6:10–17, we read that we wrestle not against flesh and blood, but against principalities and so forth. But we can say thanks be to God which giveth us the victory through our Lord Jesus Christ 1 Cor. 15:57. For the weapons are not carnal, but mighty through God to the pulling down of strong holds 2 Cor. 10:4.

Notes:

57 – Studies from the Book of Hebrews, Chapter 4

The fourth chapter of the book of Hebrews is a continuation of chapter 3, and the key word is *rest*. From verse 1, we can consider:

(a) The people for that rest—Israel Genesis 12:1–3; cf. Gen. 15:1–6.

(b) The place for that rest—Canaan—Gen. 13:14–18

(c) the principle for that rest—Faith Heb. 3:19; cf. Numbers 13:26–33.

(d) The pleasure in that rest—Satisfaction and enjoyment Numbers 13:26–27. For the believer, there is a better rest in Christ. There remaineth therefore a rest to the people of God Heb. 4:9.

(e) The people for that rest—the believers by resting in the finished work of Christ Matt. 11:28.

(f) The place or the Person in whom is that rest—Christ. Again Matt. 11:28.

(g) The principle for that rest—Faith/belief Romans 10:9–10

(h) The pleasure in that rest—Peace Romans 5:1, Joy Psalm 16:11; times of refreshing Acts 3:19; 2:38.

From verse 2 we read, for unto us was the gospel preached as well as unto them; but the word preached did not profit them, not being mixed with faith in them that heard it. The gospel means good news; Israel got the good news as to where they were going, and the faithfulness of God who will lead them there, as we can see in Exodus chapter 6:6–8, the "Seven I Wills by God":

(a) I will bring you out from under the burdens of the Egyptians;

(b) I will rid you out of their bondage;

(c) I will redeem you with a stretched out arm, and with great judgments;

(d) I will take you to me for a people;

(e) I will be to you a God: and ye shall know that I am the Lord your God, which bringeth you out from under the burdens of the Egyptians;

(f) I will bring you in unto the land concerning the which I did swear to give it to Abraham, to Isaac, and to Jacob; and

(g) I will give it you for an heritage, I am the Lord.

The gospel or good news is known as:

(a) The Gospel of God Romans 1:1. It comes from God.

(b) The Gospel of Christ Rom. 1:2. The good news is all about Christ.

(c) The Gospel of the grace of God 1 Cor; 1–2. The unmerited favor of God.

(d) The Gospel of our salvation Ephesians 1:13; 1 Corinthians 15:1–2.

Hebrews 4:3–9 tells us, "For we who have believed do enter into rest." The rest in Christ has a present enjoyment and a future hope Psalms 16:11; Eph. 3:17–19. We are not hoping to enter; we who have believed do or have entered. For there remaineth therefore a rest for the people of God.

Notes:

58 – The Atonement of Christ—Romans 5:1, 11b

Therefore being justified by faith, we have peace with God through our Lord Jesus Christ vs. 1. By whom we have now received the atonement vs. 11b.

What do we mean when we use the word *atonement*? It means to cover, to pacify, to propitiate or meeting the just demand. The word is mentioned sixteen times in Leviticus 16, the chapter that records the events on the Day of Atonement, Leviticus 16: 1-22.

On the Day of Atonement, Aaron the high priest shall come into the holy place with a young bullock for a sin offering, and a ram for a burnt-offering vs. 3. Aaron shall take of the congregation of the children of Israel two kids of the goats for a sin- offering, and one ram for a burnt-offering, vs. 5. Aaron shall offer his bullock of the sin-offering, which is for himself, and make an atonement for himself and for his house vs. 6. Aaron shall take two goats and present them before the Lord at the door of the tabernacle of the congregation vs. 7. And Aaron shall cast lots upon the two goats, one lot for the Lord, and the other lot for the scapegoat vs. 8. And Aaron shall bring the goat upon which the Lord's lot fell, and offer him for a sin-offering vs.9. But the goat on which the lot fell to be the scapegoat, shall be presented alive before the Lord, to make an atonement with him, and to let him go for a scapegoat into the wilderness vs. 10.

And Aaron shall bring the bullock of the sin-offering, which is for himself, and shall make an atonement for himself, and for his house, and shall kill the bullock of the sin-offering which is for himself vs. 11. And the bullock for the sin-offering, and the goat for the sin-offering, whose blood was brought in the make atonement in the holy place, shall one carry forth without the damp, and they shall burn in the fire their skins, and their flesh and their dung. This was the way of approach to God on the Day of Atonement according to the Levitical priesthood, and with this people can return to their homes satisfied and with a sense of relief that their sins have been dealt with until they return in another year and repeat the same ceremony In Hebrews 13:10–14 we read, We have an altar, whereof they have no right to eat which serve the tabernacle. For the bodies of those beasts, whose blood is brought into the sanctuary by the high priest for sin, are burned without the camp. Wherefore Jesus also, that he might sanctify the people with his own blood, suffered without the gate.

And in 2 Cor 3:7–9 we read, But if the ministration of death, written and engraven in stones, was glorious (They had something to be joyful about; their sins were covered for one year) so that the children of Israel could not steadfastly behold the face of Moses for the glory of his countenance, which glory was to be done away. How shall not the ministration of the spirit be rather glorious? For if the ministration of condemnation be glory, much more doth the ministration of righteousness exceed in glory?

In other words, if by their going to the Tabernacle on the Day of Atonement when the high priest will approach God on their behalf was exciting or glorious, how much more we can approach God directly through Jesus Christ who has made a once-and-for-all atonement for us? This exceeds in glory.

Therefore being justified by faith, we have peace with God through our Lord Jesus Christ vs. 1 and not only so, but we also joy in God through our Lord Jesus Christ, by whom we have now received the atonement vs. 11.The songwriter wrote:

> *Christ has for sin atonement made,*
> *what a wonderful Savior!*
> *We are redeemed! the price is paid!*
> *What a wonderful Savior!*
> *Chorus;*
> *What a wonderful Savior is Jesus my Jesus!*
> *What a wonderful Savior is Jesus my Lord!*
>
> *Redemption Song Book #103*
> *Harper Collins Publishers,*
> *77-85 Fulham Place Road, London, W6-8JB.*

Notes:

59 – The Assurance of God's Comfort and Blessing in Times of Need

As we believe the scriptures regarding God's plan and provision for us, we can then have assurance of his comfort and blessing in times of need. No matter what our circumstances may be, God is willing and able to help us. As we learn about God, we can note that God is the Supreme Being, Creator of heaven and earth. God is the all-present one who sees everything that happens to us and the world around us. God is the all-knowing one who knows all things about us and the world around us, God is the all-powerful one who has all authority and all strength. God is the all-loving one who cares and sustains us. God is love, and His love is everlasting Jeremiah 31:3. God's love is great John 15:13, and God's love is freely given Hosea 14:4.

God keeps in perfect peace all whose mind is stayed on him Isaiah 26:3. God hears our prayers and answers according to His will, His purpose, and His grace. God manifested in the flesh, in the person of Jesus Christ, and God commendeth his love toward us in that while we were yet sinners, Christ died for us Romans 5:8. Then upon our acceptance of Christ as our Savior and Lord, we become children of God Galatians 3:26.

Now, therefore, in view of the above, we can see God as our father. He is a great father and the only one to whom we must go to in times of need. Then what is your need? Is it sickness? God is the great physician Psalm 103:3. He can bring healing with or without the doctors, but we should always consult the doctor because God at times uses people to bring healing to us. Is it bereavement? God is the God of all comfort 2 Corinthians 1:3–4.

Is it finance? God is the source of all blessings. God's word says, "But my God shall supply all your needs according to His riches in glory by Christ Jesus Philippians 4:19." Is it meeting the rent or mortgage at the end of month? You may be one among many who live from paycheck to paycheck; I was one of those and had no idea how and when I would get out of it, but the Lord brought me out, praise the Lord.

Is it frustration, stress or anxiety? God cares for you. In Philippians 4:6–7 we read the words, Be careful for nothing, but in everything by prayer and supplication with thanksgiving let your request be made known unto God. And the peace of God, which passeth all understanding shall keep your heart and mind through Christ Jesus.

Is it loneliness? In Hebrews 13:5b we read these words, For He said I will never leave thee nor forsake thee, so we can say, whenever we feel lonely, God is always near. For if you put your trust in Him, you can say with the hymn writer, "I am His and He is mine." We read in Psalm 27:10, When my father and my mother forsake me, then the Lord will take me up. God by His grace will send Christian friends to stand with you, even if you did not know them before. The hymn writer said:

> *There's not a friend like the lonely Jesus,*
> *No, not one! no not one!*
> *None else could heal all our soul's diseases,*
> *No, not one! no not one!*
> *Chorus.*
> *Jesus know all about our struggles,*
> *He will guide till the day is done;*
> *There's not a friend like the lowly Jesus,*
> *No, not one! No, not one!*

Redemption Book #110,
Harper Collins Publishers,
77-85 Fulham Palace Road, London W6-8JB

Notes:

60 – *The Autobiography of Abraham, Lot, and Their Families*
Gen. 12–19

The autobiography of Abraham, Lot, and their families can be summed up in one word for each.

One word for Abraham: faithfulness—Gen 12:1–8, 18:19. God called Abraham from Haran. Get thee out of thy country, and from thy kindred, and from thy father's house, unto a land that I will shew thee. Abraham obeyed. For I know him, that he will command his children and his household after him, and they shall keep the way of the Lord, to do justice and judgment.

One word for Lot: carelessness by his separation Abraham—Gen. 13:5–9. This is known as Lot's first step in backsliding. The greatest mistake in Lot's life was his separation from his uncle Abraham. He left the place of worship and went to a land and people he did not know, and it was a wicked place (cf. the young man who was a Levite from Bethlehem-Judah, who left a place of worship and end up in the house of Micah, a man who had a house full of gods, and he was content to dwell with the man. See Judges 17:7–13). Many a young person and old ones also have been in godly homes or attending church but wander away and experience hardship because of their bad choices.

One word for the sons of Lot: heedlessness—Gen; 19:12–16. The two men that came to Lot in Sodom announcing God's judgment on that city said to Lot, Hast thou here any besides? Son-in-law, and thy sons, and thy daughters, and whatsoever thou hast in the city, bring them out of this place. For we will destroy this place, because the cry of them is waxen great before the face of the Lord, and the Lord hath sent us to destroy it. And Lot went out and spake unto his sons-in- law, which married his daughters, and said, Up, get you out of this place, for the Lord will destroy this city. But he seemed as one that mocked unto his sons-in-law.

One word for Lot's wife: worldliness—Gen. 19:24–26.The sun was risen upon the earth when Lot entered into Zoar. Then the Lord rained upon Sodom and upon Gomorrah brimstone and fire from the Lord out of heaven. And he overthrew those cities, and all the plain, and all the inhabitants of the cities, and that which grew upon the ground. But his wife looked back from behind him, and she became a pillar of salt. The Lord Jesus speaking on the context of judgment said in Luke 17:32, "Remember Lot's wife."

Are these biographies evident today? Which one fits your lifestyle?

Whatsoever was written before was written for our example that we should not live a negative lifestyle. See 1 Cor.10:6.

Notes:

CHAPTER 7

61 – The betrayal and Trial of Jesus Christ.

John 18:1-40

In Matthew 16, the Lord spoke of the church that was soon to be revealed. As He completed His statement on the church, he began to shew unto his disciples how he must go unto Jerusalem, suffer many things of the elders and chief priest and scribes, be killed, and be raised again the third day.

As we consider this as the basis upon which our salvation rest, and by which is the fundamental truth of the Christian faith, we can with grateful hearts meditate on the suffering of Christ for us. For a breakdown on what has happened we can consider:

> The Deception of Judas,
> The Delivery of Jesus,
> The Denial of Peter, and,
> The Decision of the people.

1. The Deception of Judas—John 18:1–5, cf. Matt. 26:14–16, 47–49.

    The chapter begins with the words—When Jesus had spoken these words, the words which we find in chapter 17, even at his prayer, He went forth with his disciples over the brook Kidron. Judas who knew of the place would then find and opportunity to carry out his mission, which he started with the chief priests.

2. The Delivery of Jesus John 18: 6-14.

    Jesus therefore knowing all things that should come upon him, went forth and said unto them! Whom seek ye, they said Jesus of Nazareth, Jesus said unto them I am he; And Judas also, which betrayed him, stood with them. As soon then as he had said unto them I am he, they went backward, and fell to the ground. Then ask he them again, whom seek ye? And they said Jesus of Nazareth; Jesus answered I have told you that I am he, if therefore ye seek me let these go their way.

Then the band and the captain and officers of the Jews took Jesus, and bound him, and led Him away to Annas first; for he was the father-in-law to Caiaphas, which was the high priest that same year.

3. The Denial of Peter John 18,vs. 15–18. Peter is seen to have been zealous for the Lord. He had cut of the ear of Malchus, the servant of the High Priest, according to vs. 10, but now he came in contact with the damsel that kept the door with the servants and officers, they then identified him with the One they had now arrested, even Jesus Christ, their identifying marks was by his speech: he had an accent Matt. 26:73. Peter now denied his Lord. Jesus had prayed for Peter previously, "Satan hath desire to sift you as wheat, but I have prayed for thee that thy faith fail not, and when thou are converted, strengthen thy brethren" Luke 22:31–32.

4. The Decision of the People John 18:28–38. Then led they Jesus from Caiaphas unto the hall of judgment: And it was early and they themselves went not into the Judgment hall, lest they should be defiled, but that they might eat the Passover. Pilate then went out unto them and said, what accusation bring ye against the man. Pilate saw Jesus just as another man coming before him, he called him the man (cf. 19:5): "Behold the man." Jesus was more than the man; he was the Lord Jesus Christ. Jesus told them that His kingdom is not of this world vs. 36 Pilate sought to release Jesus on his own, but because of his position, Pilate had a big problem. He could not do it, so he sought ways and means to release Christ. Pilate must go against the dictates of his own conscience, even though his wife sent unto him saying have nothing to do with this just man for I have suffered many things this day I dream because of him Matt. 27:19. But now as he had a notable prisoner Barabbas, Pilate thought he could compare Jesus with him

with the hope the multitude would agree to release Jesus instead of Barabbas, but to his disappointment they chose to release Barabbas and to crucify Jesus, John 18:39–40. The voice of the people prevailed; their charge was, If you let this man go thou art not Caesar's friend John 19:12. For a comprehensive study on the subject, read Matt 26–27, Mark 14–15, Luke 22–23, and John 18–19.

Today God wants us to make the right choice by choosing Christ as Savior and being a follower of Him. There is a song which says:

> *Jesus is standing in Pilate's hall,*
> *Friendless, forsaken, betrayed by all;*
> *Hearken, what meaneth the sudden call,*
> *What will you do with Jesus?*
> *Chorus:*
> *What will you do? what will you do?*
> *Neutral you cannot be!*
> *Someday your heart will be asking,*
> *What will He do with me!*
>
>

Redemption Song Book #701
Harper Collins Publishers,
77-85 Fulham Place Road, London, U K W6-8JB.

Notes:

62 – The Christmas Message and the Hope of Mankind

Since man fell by transgression, God made a promise of his plan for the redemption and reconciliation of mankind that we should be to the praise of his glory Eph. 1:12. With this we see:

1. The announcement of Christ—Genesis 3:15, 12:3, Isaiah 7:14, 9:6.
   The seed of the woman shall bruise the head of the serpent.
   To Abraham; In thy seed shall all the families of the earth be blessed.
   Behold a virgin shall conceive and bear a son.
   Unto us a child is born, unto us a son is given
   The government shall be on His shoulders.

2. The arrival of Christ—Matt. 2:1–5; Micah 5:2; Galatians 4:4; Luke 19:10
   The time of arrival.
   The place of arrival.
   The reason for arrival

3. The anointing of Christ—Luke 4:16–19, cf. Isaiah 61:1–2a, John 9:1–5
   To bring good news
   To open eyes of the blind
   To deliver captive sinners.

4. The atonement of Christ—Matt.27:45–53; Rom 5:11b; cf. Lev. 16.
   The death of Christ
   The dispensation of the Law
   The direction for worship.

5. The Ascension of Christ—Acts 1:8–11.

    The apostolic commission.

    The attention to His word

    The attraction to the heavens.

6. The Anticipation of Christ—Acts 1:10–11.

    The secret of his coming

    The selectiveness at his coming

    The sudden appearance at his coming.

Notes:

63 – The Last Days with Loved Ones

John 21:1–25

In everything there is a beginning and an ending, except for eternity. Jesus came into the world as a babe, born in Bethlehem, and after about thirty-three and half years, died for our sins; after this he would leave this world to return to heaven from whence he came.

In chapter 20, we see revelations on the resurrection of Christ, and in chapter 21, we can see how he spend the last few days with his disciples. We can also see the activities of the disciples during those days.

1. The preoccupation of the disciples John 21 vs. 2–3. Simon Peter said, I go fishing. They say unto him; we also go with thee. They went forth, and entered into a ship immediately, and that night they caught nothing. Their activities does not imply backsliding but rather a way of life they had prior to full-time ministries for their Lord. Their unchanging love for their master is clearly seen in the confession of Peter vs.15.

2. The partnership of the disciples with their Lord John 21 vs. 5–6. First they were on their own and caught nothing, but now Jesus is involved in their activities and gave them an instruction: "Cast the net on the right side of the ship." They did so and were not able to draw the net for the multitude of fishes. When Jesus is involved in our activities, things will always go right.

3. The preparation and dignity for the presence of the Lord John 21 vs. 7. Now when Peter heard that it was the Lord, he put on his fisher's coat unto him and did cast himself into the sea. Fishermen are not white- or blue-collar workers; they usually dress for their occupation. Peter felt he must be in a more dignified manner to meet the Master. While we must be conscious of the presence of the Lord at all times, we must consider going to church is not the same as going to the beach,

so we should be dignified. The apostle Paul gave a dress code for the Christians in 1 Timothy 2:9. He calls it modest apparel.

4. The provision for the physical needs of the disciples John 21 vs. 9–13. There was a fire of coals with fishes thereon, and an invitation to eat. "Come and dine," the master said. Jesus can always meet both our physical and spiritual needs.

5. The preference of love to the Lord Jesus against anyone else John 21 vs. 15–17. Jesus said to Peter, "Lovest thou me more than these?" Peter said yes, and an assignment was given: Feed my lambs. The second and third questions were also on commitment, and the answer was the same. Then an additional assignment was given: Feed my sheep. Why lambs, and why sheep? We know lambs are the young sheep, they need softer food; the sheep are the grown-up ones that need stronger food. As preachers and teachers, we must know how to feed.

   Peter said, As newborn babes, desire the sincere milk of the word, that ye may grow thereby 1 Peter 2:2. In Hebrews 5:12–14, we read of those who are babes in Christ and how they must be fed spiritual milk as opposed to those who are adults. Physically, we give babies milk for them to grow. We do not give a T-bone steak to a six-month-old, but we as adults do order a T-bone steak. I taught Sunday school for many years, and I love some of the Sunday school books, how the writers breakdown the lessons according to the Sunday school classes.

6. The prophetic words by Christ to Peter regarding the end-time of Peter's life, an invitation to follow Him, and advice to consider individual responsibilities and faithfulness in view of His soon coming again John 21 vs.19–25.

Notes:

64 – The Call and Promises of God by Jesus Christ

Matt. 11:28, Mk.314, Luke 10:1–9

In Genesis 12:1, the Lord said unto Abram (whose name was changed to Abraham),"Get thee out of thy country, unto a land that I will show thee. In vs. 4 Abram departed as the Lord has spoken unto him. In vs. 7 the Lord said unto Abram, unto thy seed will I give this land. That was God's call with a promise which was fulfilled by the conquest of Canaan under the leadership of Moses and Joshua Joshua 11: vs 23.

In Heb. 4:6 we read, many did not enter the Promised Land because of unbelief, had they believed, the enjoyment and the blessings according to the promise of God would have been their experiences. For in this passage we see the people for that rest, Israel, the place of that rest, the land of Canaan, but the principle for that rest is by the principle of faith, for if they had done this, we could have seen the pleasure and enjoyment in that rest they would have had.

Now Jesus said, Come unto me, I will give you rest; the people for that rest, whosoever will, the place for that rest is in Christ, and the principle for that rest is faith in the finish work of Christ, even his death burial and resurrection. Therefore, we see:

1. The call of God unto salvation Matt. 11:28. Come unto me speaks of a call from a distance to the caller, a most commonly used word for the youngest to the oldest. The C in the word *come* stands for children they to Christ must come, O stands for older ones who are called to come, M stands for middle age who also must come and E stands for everyone, everyone must come to Christ.

2. The call of God unto communion Mark 3:14. And He ordained twelve that they should be with Him; There must be time spent in communion with Christ; we may call it quiet time with Jesus, or time for devotions.

3. The call of God unto commission Mark. 3:14 that they might be with Him, and that He might send them forth to preach. The Lord who sends to preach, cf. Luke 10:1–9, sent 70 to preach two by two into every place whither He himself would come. No place in the world is out of bounds for preaching, the key word, whither He himself would come, if the Lord would go there, then he would want us to go there also. We may not be much, we may not have many workers, but notice that there was only seventy sent to the multitude of people. We can think of:

(a) The nucleus of the laborers—few

(b) The need of the hour—now

(c) The nature of the assignment—sheep among wolves, but

(d) The nearness of the Savior—Lo I am with you Matt. 28:19–20.

4. The call unto consecration ref: Gen. 35:1. We must be in good fellowship with God; to be used by God, sin must be confessed and put away. Jacob left Shechem unto the place which he had called Bethel Gen. 28:12–22. Now in Gen. 35:1, God said unto Jacob, arise, go up to Bethel, and dwell there, and make there and altar. Jacob then said unto his household; Put away the strange gods that are among you, and be clean, and change your garments, And let us arise, and go up to Bethel, vs. 4. And they gave unto Jacob all the strange gods which were in their hands, and all their earrings which were in their ears, and Jacob hid them under the oak which was by Shechem. Jacob got rid of those things not pleasing to God vs. 6. So Jacob came to Luz, which is in the land of Canaan, that is, Bethel, he and all the people that were with him.

Notes:

65 – The Call and Commission of Moses

Exodus 3:4–23

1. The circumstances surrounding Moses were such that Moses was feeding the flock of Jethro his father-in-law Exodus 3:1–2. Now Moses kept the flock of Jethro his father in law, the priest of Midian, and he led the flock to the backside of the desert and came to the mountain of God, even to Horeb. And the angel of the Lord appeared unto him in a flame of fire out of the midst of a bush: And he looked, and, behold, the bush burned with fire, and the bush was not consumed.

2. The call of God to Moses Exodus 3 vs. 4–6. God called him by name. Sometimes God call us individually for a specific assignment; we may not at all times understand when God calls a person and for what, so we must not be too quick to discourage them; instead pray for that person.

3. The commission of God for Moses Exodus 3 vs. 7–10. The commission was direct, and the people were identified; it was Israel in bondage at Egypt. The Lord said I have surely seen the affliction of my people which are in Egypt, and have heard their cry by reason of their taskmasters, for I know their sorrows and I am come down to deliver them out of the hand of the Egyptians, and to bring them up out of that land unto a good land and a large, unto a land flowing with milk and honey, unto the place of the Canaanites, and the Hittites and the Amorites, and the Perizzites, and the Hivites, and the Jebusites.

    Exodus 3 vs. 10 God said to Moses "Come now therefore, and I will send thee unto Pharaoh, that thou mayest d bring forth the children of Israel out of Egypt" We may note that if God gives a commission, he will give the enablement and the provision. God gave

Moses the comfort and encouragement. Certainly I will be with thee, and this shall be a token unto thee, that I have sent thee.

4. The complaint to God by Moses Exodus 3 vs. 11–12. Moses said unto God, Who am I, that I should go unto Pharaoh, and that I should bring forth the children of Israel out of Egypt. When thou hast brought forth the people out of Egypt, ye shall serve God upon this mountain..

Notes:

66 – The Church of Our Lord Jesus Christ

Matt. 16:13–18

The church of our Lord Jesus Christ is known as a called-out assembly. Israel is referred to as the church in the wilderness Acts 7:37–38. Israel was a called-out assembly only while they were in the wilderness; from the time they came into the land of Canaan they have been known as the nation of Israel.

In Matt. 16:13–18, our Lord Jesus said, I will build my church. This implies that His church was not yet manifested, but would be in the not-too-distant future after his statement, for during the time of his public ministry, man was under the Dispensation of the Law. Therefore we can see:

1. The promise of the Church vs. 18 I will build my church.
2. The presence of the Church Acts 2:1–47. This is after the death, burial, and resurrection of Christ. I will have a called-out assembly when 120 people including His earthly mother and brethren gathered and prayed Acts 1:14. His brothers according to the flesh did not believe at first, but afterward, they did John 7:1–5.
3. The program of the Church Matt. 26:26; John 12:3–8; John 4:20–23; Matt; 28:19–20; 1 Thess; 1:8–10; 2 Tim. 4:1–2—Worshiping the Lord and witnessing to the world. The Lord gave the example and instructions for worship and witnessing; the apostles gave the methods for worship and witness. There the program is simple and relevant for every age.
4. The practice of the program of the church; Acts 20:7. And upon the first day of the week when he disciples came together to break bread, Paul preached unto them ready to depart on the morrow, and continued his speech until midnight, they did what they were taught by the Lord in Matt. 26:26–29, Luke 22:19–20. This do in remembrance of me;

by doing this on the first day of the week shows the remembrance of the death, burial, and resurrection of the Lord Jesus, for before the first day of the week He was in the grave, so we cannot remember all three if it is not on the first day of the week. Also the Holy Spirit came on the first day of the week.

5. The protection and preservation of the Church Matthew16 vs. 18; John 10:27–30. Jesus said, I will build my church and the gates of hell shall not prevail against it—or the worst thing you can think of that will happen to the church would not prevent it from functioning until I come for it. My sheep hear my voice, and I know them, and they follow me. And I give unto them eternal life, and they shall never perish, neither shall any man pluck them out of my hand. My father which gave them me is greater than all and no man is able to pluck them out of my Father's hand. I and my Father are one.

6. The prospect and anticipation of the Church 1 Thess. 4:13–18. The apostle said, But I would not have you to be ignorant, brethren, concerning them which are asleep, that ye sorrow not, even as others which have no hope. For if we believe that Jesus died and rose again even so them also which sleep in Jesus will God bring with him. For this we say unto you by the word of the Lord, that we which are alive and remain unto the coming of the Lord shall not prevent or (precede) them which are asleep. For the Lord himself shall descend from heaven with a shout, with the voice of the archangel, and with the trump of God; and the dead in Christ shall rise first. Then we which are alive and remain shall be caught up together with them in the clouds, to meet the Lord in the air, and so shall we ever be with the Lord. Wherefore comfort one another with these words.

7. The pleasure of the Church Ephesians 5:25–27. Husbands are exhorted to love their wives even as Christ also love the church and gave himself for it. That he might sanctify and cleanse it with the washing of water by the word vs. 27. That he might present it to Himself a glorious

church, not having spot, or wrinkle or any such thing, but that it should be holy and without blame.

8. The perfection of the Church Jude 24–25. We do not teach sinless perfection now, for we do make mistakes, though we should not sin presumptuously. However, when we realize we have sinned, we should go to 1 John 1:9: If we confess our sins, He is faithful and just to forgive us our sins, and to cleanse us from all unrighteousness. Then according to Jude 24–25, we read, Now unto him that is able to keep you from falling, and to present you faultless before the presence of his glory with exceeding joy. To the only wise God our Savior be glory and majesty, dominion, and power, both now and ever. The songwriter says:

> *When in heaven I see thy glory,*
> *When before thy throne I bow,*
> *Perfected I shall be like Thee,*
> *Fully thy redemption know.*
> *Chorus.*
> *My Redeemer, My Redeemer*
> *Then shall hear me shout His praise*
> > *Believers Hymn Book #159*
> > *Author's Name not mentioned, but sold at John Richie*
> > *LTD,Kilmarnock, Scotland/*

Notes:

67 – The Crucifixion and Resurrection of Christ
John 19:1–37; 20:1–31

The chapter begins with the words: Then Pilate therefore took Jesus and scourged him vs. 1. Pilate then said "Behold the man" vs. 5, but in verse 14 Pilate said, Behold your king. Could it be that Pilate then had a better understanding of Christ? Even then he was rejected, and they cried out, Away with Him, away with him, crucify him, crucify him. John 19–15.

Then delivered he him therefore unto them to be crucified; And they took Jesus, and led him away outside the city John 19 vs. 16–20, this being in fulfillment to the type of Christ in Lev. 16:27 according to Heb. 13:11–12. For the bodies of those beasts, whose blood is brought into the sanctuary by the high priest for sins are burned without the camp; Wherefore, Jesus also, that he might sanctify the people with his own blood suffered without the gate Heb. 13:11–12.

Now we can hear the seven last words of Christ on the cross:

1. My God, My God why hast thou forsaken me Matt. 27:46? Scorned by man, by God forsaken outside the camp.
2. Father forgive them for they know not what they do Luke 23:34. The compassion of Christ on them.
3. Today shall thou be with me in paradise Luke 23:43. The compassion of Christ to them.
4. Father into thine hand I commit my spirit, Luke 23:46. Not my will but Thine.
5. Woman behold thy son John 19:26. What a sight.
6. I thirst John 19:28. The agony of Christ.
7. It is finished John 19:20. The completion of His work for our salvation.

The end of chapter 19 presents the record on the death and burial of Christ. Now in chapter 20 we learn of the amazing discoveries on the resurrection of Christ.

1. The discovery of the women who saw how he was buried, but now the open tomb Matt. 28:1, Mark 16:1–6, Luke 224:1–10, John 20:1.
2. The discovery of the other disciple who did outrun Peter and the linen clothes vs. 3–5.
3. The discovery of Peter who went into the sepulcher. The Napkin wrapped together in a place by itself vs. 5–7
4. The discovery of Mary who stayed by the sepulcher. The two Angels and Jesus Himself vs. 11–16.
5. The departure of Jesus—Where? To the Father and our God vs. 17.The songwriter said:

> *Rise my soul behold tis Jesus,*
> *Jesus fills thy wandering eyes,*
> *See Him now in glory seated,*
> *where thy sins no more can rise*
> *There in righteousness transcendent,*
> *Lo! He doth in heaven appear.*
> *Shows the blood of His atonement;*
> *As thy title to be there*
>
> *The Believers Hymn Book #238*
> *Author J.Denham Smith Sold by John Ritchie Ltd.*
> *Kilmarnock, Scotland.*

Notes:

68 – The Coming of Christ for His church, and the coming of Christ with His Church

1 Thess. 4:13–18, 1 Cor. 15:51–57, Matt. 24:29–30, Rev. 1:7, Rev. 19:11–16; 13:16–17, Isaiah 9:6–7, 2 Samuel 7:8–17, Dan. 7:25; 9:27, 2 Thess. 2:1–2, Luke 21; 24, Rev. 6:10—11:68

The subject of the church is in two parts: Christ building and coming for his Church in the air. And Christ coming with his Church known as the Revelation of Christ when He comes to establish His earthly kingdom; between these two events there will be seven years, these studies can be extensive, but with patience we will understand the whole matter on the subject.

In Isaiah 9:6 we read:

For unto us a child is born, unto us a son is given: and the government shall be upon His shoulder; and his name shall be called, Wonderful, Counselor, the mighty God, The everlasting Father, the Prince of peace. Of the increase of his government and peace there shall be no end, upon the throne of David, and upon his kingdom to order it, and to establish it with judgment and with justice from henceforth even forever.

This fulfilling the prophecy of the Davidic Covenant 2nd Samuel 23:5. and bringing an end to the four great gentile world empires, from Nebuchadnezzar in Babylon to the Antichrist, when times of the Gentiles will be fulfilled. Luke 21:24.

What will precede the Revelation of Christ after the coming for his Church?:According to the prophecy of Daniel 70th week or 490 years in Daniel 9:27, there will be seven years between the coming of Christ for the Church and the coming of Christ with his Church. What will happen in this seven years? There will be a great super political personality known as the Antichrist, see 2 Thess. 2:1–12, and just after the rapture of the Church, he will make a covenant or as it were a peace treaty with Israel for seven years, which is the last week of the seventy weeks of years prophecy, but in the midst of the week or 3 ½ years he will break the covenant and he will set up his image in Jerusalem and have the entire world be dominated by his power, so that no one will be able to buy or sell 2 Thess. 2:1–12, Rev. 13:16–17. Those who were not in the church of Jesus Christ will suffer as never before, and this will be for another 3 ½ years. There will be the cry, How long O Lord, and it would be said until a time, times and the dividing of a time. Time is one year, Times are two years and the dividing of a time is six months, which is 3 ½ years. This will fulfill the seventy weeks or 490 years of Daniel's prophecy. What next?

How would the Revelation of Christ be?

Immediately after the Tribulation of those days shall the Sun be darkened, the moon shall not give her light, the stars shall fall from heaven. And then shall appear the sign of the Son of Man in heaven, coming in the clouds of heaven with power and great glory. Matt. 24:29–30. Behold he cometh with clouds and every eye shall see him and they also which pierced him and all kindreds of the earth shall wail because of Him. Rev. 1:7

More of this in our study on the dispensations, but from this study we can see it is very important to believe on the Lord Jesus Christ now and be in his church before it's too late. A songwriter wrote:

> *When Jesus comes to reward his servants;*
> *Whether it be noon or night!*
> *Faithful to Him He will find us watching;*
> *With our lamps all trimmed and bright?*
> *Chorus;*
> *Oh, can we say we are ready, brother...*
> *Ready for the soul's bright home?*
> *Say, will He find you and me still watching,*
> *Waiting, waiting, when the Lord shall come?*
>
> *Redemption Song Book:*
> *by Harper Collins Publishers*
> *77-85 Fulham Place Road, London W6-8JB.*

Notes:

69 – The Spiritual Meaning of God's Creation

2 Cor 4:6–18, 1 Thess 5:4–5, Gen. 1 1–31, 2:1–3.

*F*or God who commanded the light to shine out of darkness, hath shined in our hearts, to give the light of the knowledge of the glory of God in the face of Jesus Christ 2 Cor. 4:6.

When did God cause the light to shine? In the first day of creation, God said; Let there be light and there was light. The same God who cause the light to shine out of darkness, the same God hath shined in our hearts, because there is only one God, 2nd Cor.4:6 But how did the light shine in our hearts, and what has been the result? For the answer, we must consider that there are three persons in the Godhead known as the Triune God: the Father, Son, and Holy Spirit yet one God. In Genesis 1:26, God said Let us make man (plural), and in Genesis 1:27 we read, and God created man in His own image (singular). In Deut 6:4 Moses said Hear O Israel the Lord our God is one God.

In Genesis 1:2b–3 we read, And the Spirit of God moved upon the face of the waters. And God said "Let there be light and there was light." In Joel 2:28–29 God said:

And it shall come to pass afterward, that I will pour out my spirit upon all flesh, (meaning upon all mankind), and your sons and your daughters shall prophesy, and your old men shall dream dreams, your young men shall see visions. And also upon the servants and upon the handmaids in those days will I pour out my spirit.

This was quoted by the Apostle Peter on the Day of Pentecost when 3,000 people responded to his preaching, bringing about the beginning of the Church of our Lord Jesus Christ with 3,000 people plus 120 who were already in an upper room Acts 1:13; 2:41 This was through the work of the Holy spirit, the three persons of the Godhead.

How did it happen? In John 14:16 Jesus said:

"I will pray the Father, and he shall give you another Comforter, that he may abide with you forever; Even the Spirt of truth, whom the world cannot receive because it seeth him not, neither knoweth him, but ye know him for he dwelleth with you and shall be in you. There Jesus spoke of the Holy Spirit."

In John 16:7 Jesus said Nevertheless l tell you the truth, It is expedient for you that I go away, for if I go not away, the Comforter will not come unto you, but if I depart I will send him unto you. And when he is come he will reprove the world of sin, and of righteousness and of judgment.

So what is the work of the Holy Spirit to bring someone into the Church of God? (1) He reprove or enlightens one of his sins and his need of a Savior John 16:13-14, cf. Heb. 6:4–5. (2) He reveals the person and work of Christ to him, that is, Christ died for our sins, was buried, and rose again. And (3) He gives that person an impulse to receive Christ as his savior. If that person responds positively and receives Christ as his savior, instantly the Holy Spirit comes in and dwells in that person, Instantly that person is removed from a state of darkness to God's marvelous light, and this is done by the Holy Spirit as that person puts his/her faith in Christ.

Now therefore we are children of light and not children of darkness 1 Thess. 5:5. Remember on the day of Pentecost there might have been plenty more people when Peter preached, but the number 3,000 is recorded as those who responded.

For God who commanded the light to shine out of darkness hath shined in our hearts, to give the light of the knowledge of the glory of God in the face of Jesus Christ 2 Cor. 4:6. Now that we have been saved by the grace of God, we must now tell others of the Savior we have found. For more on the spiritual meaning of God's creation, we can see:

Day 1 Light. The Spirit of God moved and God said let there be light and there was light type of salvation to the one who believes the gospel.

Day 2 Firmament. God made the firmament and divided the waters which were under the firmament Type of separation from sin. A new creature in Christ 2 Cor. 5:17.

Day 3 Plant life. God said let the earth bring forth grass, the herb yielding seed and the fruit tree yielding fruit. Production. Everyone who is born again should bring forth fruit unto God. The fruit of the Spirit is love, joy, etc. Gal. 5:22–23.

Day 4. Sun and Moon. God said Let there be lights in the firmament of the heaven. This speaks of our shining in this world; Jesus said let your light so shine among men that they may see your good works and glorify your Father which is in heaven. It is said the moon is a dark object, but it reflect its light from the sun. We have no light in ourselves, so our reflection comes by our relationship and fellowship of with Christ who is the light of the world.

Day 5. The Waters bring forth abundantly. God said Let the waters bring forth abundantly moving creature that hath life. God said be fruitful and multiply.

Multiplication. We have the command to make disciples by proclaiming the truth of the gospel or duplicate ourselves.

Day 6. God said let us make man in our image, after our likeness. So God created man in his own image, in the image of God created he them male and female created he them Gen 1:26–27. This is the last of God's creation. Completion. There will be the end time of our labors. The Apostle Paul said, I have fought a good fight, I have finished my course 2nd Timothy 4:7

Day 7. Thus the heaven and the earth were finished and all the host of them. And on the seventh day God ended his work. And God rested on the 7th day. Gen. 2. 1–2. This speaks of our eternal rest. Blessed are the dead which die in the Lord from hence forth, Yea, saith the spirit, that they may rest from their labors, and their works do follow them Rev. 14:13. In all six days of creation there was an evening and a morning, but for the seventh day there was no evening or morning mentioned because it speaks of eternity when there is no end.

Notes:

70 – The Day of Opportunity
Luke 13:22–25, Matt. 7:13–14, Mark 10:17–22, 23–26, Jeremiah 8:20

There is a saying: Opportunity knocks but once; another saying says Lost opportunity can never be regained. Therefore it is important that we give earnest heed to opportunities which present themselves to us. Now in this passages we can study:

1. The Urgency of Salvation: Luke 13:22–25. And Jesus went through the cities and villages, teaching and journeying toward Jerusalem. Then said one unto Him, Are there few that be saved? And he said unto them, Strive to enter in at the straight gate: for many, I say unto you will seek to enter in and shall not be able. When once the master of the house is risen up, and hath shut the door, and ye begin to stand without, and to knock at the door, saying Lord, Lord, open unto us; and he shall answer and say unto you, I know you not whence ye are.

2. The Dependency for Salvation: In Mark 10:17–22 we read: And when he was gone forth into the way, there came one running, and kneeled to him, and asked him Good Master, what shall I do that I may inherit eternal life? Good, he realized the urgency of salvation. Jesus pointed him to the Ten Commandments, and he said, all these have I observed from my youth. Jesus pointed him to his wealth, he was not prepared to part with some of it to get what he asked for, which was eternal life. He went away sorrowful. He was dependent on something else than what he Lord had to offer.

3. The Complacency about Salvation, not in a hurry, plenty of time. In Jeremiah 8:20 we read, The harvest is past, the summer is ended and we are not saved. In 2 Cor. 6:2 we read, Behold now is the accepted time, behold now is the day of salvation. However, in Jeremiah 8:21, the question was asked: Is there no balm in Gilead, is there no physician there? Why then is not the health of the daughter of my

people recovered? In other words, is there no hope; are all hopes gone? There is a chorus with these words

> *There is a balm in Gilead*
> *To make the wounded whole... Yes.*
> *There is a balm in Gilead,*
> *To save the sin sick soul.*

Notes:

CHAPTER 8

71 – The Only Lost Opportunity That Can Never Be Regained

Acts 24:24–25

The apostle Paul was saved by the grace of God Acts 9, committed to the work of the Lord, and commended to the service of the Lord Acts 13:1–3. During the time of his ministry he was apprehended and brought before kings and governors for the sake of the gospel.

In Acts 24:24–25 we read, and after certain days, when Felix came with his wife Drusilla, which was a Jewess, he sent for Paul, and heard him concerning the faith in Christ. And as he reasoned of righteousness, temperance, and judgment to come, Felix trembled and answered, go thy way for this time when I have a convenient season, I will call for thee. He did not say get lost, but for this time, the watch word said procrastination is the thief of time. The apostle did not argue, for when there is an argument, no one wins or get their message across, and it seems that the Apostle Paul was just calm, cool, and collected.

1. Paul reasoned on righteousness, meaning one must be right with God. In Job 25:4 Bildad ask one of the most profound questions: How then can a man be justified with God? Or how can he be clean that is born of a woman? Or how can man be right with God. This question was answered in Acts 13:38 by the apostle Paul: Be it known unto you therefore, men and brethren, that through this man (Jesus Christ) is preached unto you the forgiveness of sins, and by him all that believe are justified from all things, from which ye could not be justified by the law of Moses.

2. Paul reasoned on temperance, meaning self-control; sometimes we say, don't let your mind run out of control, have discipline of the mind,

and stay focused on the important subject to obtain righteousness, and then;

3. Paul reasoned on the judgment to come. By this time Governor Felix knew what Paul was talking about, he knew it was a serious matter, he knew it's a time he must face, and he knew there are serious consequences to the reality of that judgment Paul was talking about, so he trembled. We do not know what impact the message had on his wife, but she got the same message as her husband.

There are five judgments mentioned in the New Testament;

(1) The judgment for sin John 12:31–33.
(2) The judgment by the believer 1 Cor. 11:31
(3) The judgment for the believer 2 Cor. 5:10; this judgment is like an award ceremony for our service here since we have been saved.
(4) The judgment of the nations Matt. 25. 31–41 and
(5) The Great White Throne Judgment Rev. 20:12

We believe this is the one Paul was referring to when Governor Felix trembled, for this one is the most frightening of all. We believed Governor Felix understood it all when he trembled and said go thy way for this time; when I have a convenient season, I will call for thee, but we never read governor Felix received Christ as Savior, even though he sent for Paul oftener and communed with him until two years when he left office.

Notes:

72 – The Incomparable and Incomprehensible Love of God

Exodus 21:1–6, 2 Samuel 9:1–26

Love is defined as a strong affection, and as related to God's love we see:

God's love is universal, John 3:16 says, For God so love the world. God's love is everlasting Jeremiah 31:3. God's love is freely given Hosea 14:4; God's love is great John 15:13. Behold what manner of love the Father hath bestowed upon us, that we should be called the sons of God 1 John 3:1. God's love is seen demonstrated in the lives of many as examples to follow.

1. The slave/Master relationship Exodus. 21:1–6 Now these are the judgments which thou shall set before them. If thou buy an Hebrew servant, six years he shall serve; and the seventh he shall go out free for nothing. If he came in by himself, he shall go out by himself: if he were married, then his wife shall go out with him. If his master have given him a wife, and she have born him sons or daughters, the wife and her children shall be her master's, and he shall go out by himself. And if the servant shall plainly say, I love my master, my wife, and my children; I will not go out free: Then his master shall bring him unto the judges, he shall also bring him to the door, or unto the door post, and his master shall bore his ear through with an aul; (an Aul is something shoe repairers would use to bore the leather, like a big needle with a handle, my father had one) and he (the slave) shall serve his master forever. This was the expression of great love by a slave.

2. Jonathan/David. 2 Samuel 1:23–26. The relationship and love between Jonathan and David was so strong, their love passeth the love of women vs. 26.

   Jonathan saved David when his father Saul wanted to kill David. When David then came to the throne, he could not return the love to

Jonathan because both he and his father King Saul died in the battle with the Philistines 1 Sam. 31. So now in 2 Samuel 9:1–13, David would now repay the kindness of Jonathan to his son Mephibosheth, (a very touching story).

3. Now David said, Is there yet any that is left of the house of Saul, that I may shew him kindness for Jonathan's sake? And there was of the house of Saul a servant whose name was Ziba. And when they had called him unto David, the king said unto him, art thou Ziba? And he said, Thy servant is he. And the king said, Is there not yet any of the house of Saul, that I may shew the kindness of God unto him? And Ziba said unto the king, Jonathan hath yet a son, which is lame on his feet. vs4. And the king said unto him, Where is he? And Ziba said unto the king, Behold, he is in the house of Machir, the son of Ammiel, in Lo-debar. Then King David sent and fetched him out the house of Machir, the son of Ammiel, from Lo-debar. Verse 6 says, now when Mephibosheth, the son of Jonathan, the son of Saul, was come unto David, he fell on his face, and did reverence. And David said, Mephibosheth; And he answered, Behold thy servant. In this story we see

    1. Mephibosheth: The Unhealthy Beneficiary, lame on his feet vs. 3. Man is spiritually sick from the sole of the foot even unto the head Isaiah. 1:6.

    2. Mephibosheth: The Unworthy Recipient 2nd Samuel 9 vs. 8 Man is totally unworthy of the least of God's mercies because of sin cf Genesis 33:10

    3. Mephibosheth: had Unlimited Supplies vs. 10. Besides Mephibosheth eating at David's table, His servant Ziba had fifteen sons and twenty servants working for him (thirty-five people).

        The believer also has unlimited supplies. Phil 4:19 says, But my God shall supply all you need according to his riches in glory by Christ Jesus.

4. Mephibosheth had an Unbroken Relationship with David 2nd Samuel 9 vs. 11. Whereas the believer may have a broken fellowship with the Lord by not walking worthy of our calling unto holiness, the believer has an unbroken relationship with God, once we receive Christ as Savior John 5:24, John 10:27–28, 1 Peter 1:5. All these are known as the eternal security of the child of God.

Notes:

73 – The End of Time: How Shall We Be Affected?

2 Thess. 2:1–12, Gen. 49:10, Lev. 8:1–4.

Second Thess 1:1–2 begins: Paul, and Silvanus, and Timotheus, unto the Church of the Thessalonians in God our Father and the Lord Jesus Christ. Grace unto you, and peace, from God our Father and the Lord Jesus Christ.

Now we beseech you, brethren, by the coming of our Lord Jesus Christ, and by our gathering, together unto him. That ye be not soon shaken in mind, or be troubled, neither by spirit, nor by word, nor by letter as form us, as that day of Christ is at hand. Let no man deceive you by any means, for that day shall not come, except there comes a falling away first, and that man of sin be revealed, the son of perdition 2:1–3. From these verses we see:

1. The information relating to the end time or the coming of our Lord Jesus Christ to set up His earthly kingdom 2 Thess 2:1 There will be a gathering unto Him; has there been any gathering unto him mentioned before? Is there any gathering unto him now? And would there be a gathering unto him in the future? In Genesis 49:10 we read, "The Scepter shall not depart from Judah, nor a lawgiver from between his feet, until Shiloh come; and unto him shall the gathering of the people be. Who is the "him" who shall gather the people?

    In Leviticus 8:1–4 after the tabernacle was completed, God asked Moses to take Aaron and his sons with him, and the garments, and the anointing oil and a bullock for the sin-offering, and two rams, and a basket of unleavened bread; And that he must gather all the congregation together unto the door of the tabernacle of the congregation. Here we find the whole congregation was around Aaron, was this the fulfilment of Genesis 49:10? No, for Aaron was from the tribe of Levi and the one unto whom the gathering will be, would be from the tribe of Judah. Therefore in Heb. 7:14 we read, Our Lord (according to the flesh) sprang out from the tribe of Judah, the one referred to in Gen. 49:10, the one around whom the gathering of the people would be, this to be fulfilled in the future according to 2 Thess. 2:1–3.

However, is there a gathering unto him today—yes. When each local church comes together for worship and praise, we are gathered unto Him, who alone is worthy of our worship and praise, and Jesus himself said in Matt. 18:20, Where two or three are gathered together in my name, there am I in the midst of them. This is a present gathering unto Him. However; there will be a future gathering unto Him according to 2 Thess. 2:1, and that will be after the rapture of the Church 1 Thess. 4:13–18; therefore before this future gathering unto Him we can see the incredible things that will take place 2 Thess. Chapter 2 vs.4–8. One will arise who opposeth and exalteth himself above all that is called God or one that will oppose every form of worship to God, and exalt himself in the temple of God, he is known as the Antichrist, he will legislate and execute all form of lawlessness and force everyone to receive his mark on their forehead, but we see as of this present time he is restrained from being manifested. Why? Verse 7 said only he who now letteth will let until he is taken out of the way. Or Only He the Holy Spirit who now hinders will continue to hinder until He is taken out of the way. When will the Holy Spirit be taken out of the way that this man of sin be revealed; Each believer in Christ has the Holy Spirit in him or her, so when Christ comes for the Church at the rapture and we all are gone the Holy Spirit who is in us will also be gone, taken out of the way, and then that man of sin (the Antichrist) shall be revealed, whom the Lord shall consume with the spirit of his mouth, and shall destroy with the brightness of his coming, even him, whose coming is after the working of Satan with all power and signs and lying wonders. What a sad day that will be?

That is why we read in 2 Cor. 6:2, "Behold now is the accepted time, behold now is the day of salvation. One must accept Christ as savior now because Christ can come anytime.

2. The insecurity of the people who failed to accept Christ as Savior 2nd Thess. vs. 9–12. And with all deceivableness of unrighteousness in them that perish, because they received not the love of the truth, that they might be saved. And for this cause God shall send them strong delusion, that they should believe a lie, that they all might be damned who believed not the truth, but had pleasure in unrighteousness. The songwriter said:

> O Sinner, the savior is calling for thee,
> Long, long has He call thee in vain;
> He called the when joy lent it crown to thy days,
> He called thee in sorrow and pain;
> Chorus:
> Oh, turn while the Savior in mercy is waiting,
> And steer for the harbor light;
> For how do you know that your soul may be drifting,
> Over the dead-line to-night
>
> *Redemption Song Book #230*
> *Harper Collins Publishers,*
> *77-85 Fulham Palace Road, London W6-8JB*

Notes:

74 – The Fruitful Life of Samuel

1 Samuel 12:1–15

In chapter 8 we see that Israel rejected the Lord God as their king and desired a king whom they can see so that they can be like all other nations—that is world conformity. Samuel told them of the king they will have in chapter 8 vs. 11–18, but in verse 19 they said, Nay but we will have a king over us. When there is rebellion and determination, God sometimes allows one to have his way, according to the permissible will of God against the direct will of God. In chapter 11, vs. 15, Israel went to Gilgal and made Saul king before the Lord. Now in chapter 12 we see:

1. The testimony of Samuel regarding his faithfulness to the Lord, chapter 12 vs. 1–5:

    And Samuel said unto all Israel, Behold I have hearkened unto your voice in all that ye said, unto me, and have made a king over you. And now, behold the king walketh before you: and I am old and grayheaded; and behold, my sons are with you: and I have walked before you from my childhood unto this day.

    Behold, here I am: witness against me before the Lord, and before his anointed: whose ox have I taken? 1st Samuel 12:3 or whose donkey have I taken? 1st Samuel 12:3, Or whom have I defrauded? Whom have I oppressed? Or of whose hand have I received any bribe to blind mine eyes therewith? And I will restore it.

2. The testimony and confirmation regarding the testimony of Samuel, 1st Samuel 12 vs. 4–5:

    And they said, Thou hast not defrauded us, nor oppressed us, neither hast thou taken ought of any man's hand. The Lord is witness.

3. The testimony of Samuel as to the grace and righteousness of God, in His dealing with Israel from Egypt to Canaan. Then challenge them

that they should obey and faithfully follow the Lord chapter 12 vs. 6–15.

For an application to this we can consider these passages in the New Testament:

Regarding the need for faithfulness to the Lord; we can consider these references.

Holding fast our profession of faith Heb.10:23
Holding faith and a good conscience 1 Tim. 1:19
Holding forth the word of God Phil. 2:16
Holding fast the faithful word Titus 1:9
Holding fast till I come Rev. 2:25.

Notes:

75 – The Life and Works of Jonah, God's Prophet to Nineveh
Jonah chapters 1–3

Jonah is seen in the book of Jonah as the servant of the Lord who tried to do what he wanted to do, but it could be said that you can't run away from God.

In these chapters we see:

1. Jonah: The disobedient prophet, running away from God. In Jonah 1:1–17 God said to Jonah arise and go to Nineveh, that great city and cry against it, but Jonah did not want to go where God sent him, he was disobedient, so he thought of a plan that would allow him to have his way, that is to go to Tarshish from the presence of the Lord, so he went down to Joppa, found a ship going to Tarshish, and he would do everything legal, so he paid the fare, and went down into the ship to go with them unto Tarshish from the presence of the Lord. But what happened as a result of Jonah's disobedience.

    The Lord sent out a great wind into the sea, and there was mighty tempest in the sea, so that the ship was like to be broken. Jonah caused the mariners to be afraid, and cried every man unto his god, cast forth the cargo into the sea, to lighten the ship, and despite of the difficulties, Jonah gone down into the sides of the ship, and he lay, and was fast asleep, nothing moved Jonah 1:1–5. The shipmaster came to him, and said unto him, What meanest thou, O sleeper? Arise, call upon thy God, if so be that God will think upon us, that we perish not. We now see the determination of the people to find out the cause of their problem by casting lots, and the lot fell on Jonah. Now that he is found out, he confessed, acknowledging his sins, and suggested that they cast him into the sea, where he was swallowed by a great fish prepared by the Lord. And Jonah was in the belly of the fish three days and three nights vs. 17. It is a serious thing to disobey God. In 1 Samuel 15:22 we read, to obey is better than sacrifice.

2. Jonah: the Praying Prophet. Running back to God. Chapter 2. Jonah acknowledged his mistake and disobedience, he prayed unto Lord his God out of the belly of the fish and said, I cried by reason of mine affliction unto the Lord out of the belly of hell cried I, and thou heardest my voice, 2:1–2. In Psalm 46:1 we read, God is our refuge and strength, a very present help in times of trouble. Even though we have caused the trouble vs. 4. Jonah said I am cast out of thy sight, yet I will look again toward they holy temple vs. 9. Jonah said salvation is of the Lord vs. 10. And the Lord spake unto the fish, and it vomited out Jonah upon the dry land.

3. Jonah: The Faithful Prophet Running with God chapter 3: vs. 1.
    The word of the Lord came unto Jonah the second time, saying Arise, go God to Nineveh, that great city and preach unto it the preaching that I bid thee. So Jonah arose, and went unto Nineveh, according to the word of the Lord. Note the same call, unto the same place with the same commission, for the same reason. Sometimes God speaks to us, but we are disobedient. By God's grace, he gives us a second chance to accomplish the same mission, but by going our own way we can have serious experiences: waste of time, and many sorrow and emotional stresses. Had we obeyed God at first we would have been saved from these experiences. And, yes we would accomplish the mission but with experiences we could have avoided. Israel spent forty years in the wilderness because of disobedience.

However, according to vs. 4, we give Jonah credit for being obedient to the second call from God. Jonah began to enter into the city of Nineveh, a day's journey, when he carried, and said, "Yet forty days and Nineveh shall be overthrown, chapter 3 vs. 5–10. We see the impact of his message on the people of Nineveh, from the greatest to the least of them. For the word came unto the king of Nineveh, and he arose from his throne, and laid his robe from him, covered himself with sackcloth, and sat in ashes, (evidence of repentance). And then decree legislation that the whole city turn to God vs. 10. And God saw their works, that they turned from their evil way, and God repented of the evil, that he had said he would do unto them, and he did it not. All because Jonah the faithful prophet was now running with God.

Application: It is very important to answer the call of God, whether for salvation of for service and for salvation.

> The songwriter said:
> *I've wandered far away from God,*
> *Now I'm coming home;*
> *The path of sin too long I've trod,*
> *Lord I'm coming home.*
> *Chorus:*
> *Coming home, coming home,*
> *Never more to roam;*
> *Open wide Thine arms of love,*
> *Lord I'm coming home.*
> *Redemption Song Book # 268,*
> *Harper Collins Publishers, 77-85 Fulham Palace Road,*
> *London W6-8JB.*

Notes:

76 – The Life of Joseph as a Type of Christ
Genesis Chapters 37 through 41

Joseph, the son of Jacob whose name was changed to Israel, lived with his parents in the land of Canaan. At the age of seventeen he was feeding the flock with his brothers and brought to his father reports on their evil deeds. Israel loved Joseph more than all his children because he was the son of his old age, and Israel made Joseph a coat of many colors. When Joseph's brethren saw that their father loved Joseph more than themselves, they hated him and could not speak peaceable to him. Therefore in this chapter we can see:

1. Joseph; Beloved of the father, Gen. 37:3. His father made him a coat of many colors.
2. Joseph; Hated by his brethren, Gen. 37:4. They could not speak peaceably to him.
3. Joseph; Conspired against by his brethren Gen. 37:18. And when they saw him afar off, even before he came near unto them, they conspired against him to kill him.
4. Joseph; Stripped out of his coat Gen. 37:23. And it came to pass, when Joseph was come unto his brethren, that they stript him out of his coat, his coat of many colors that was on him.
5. Joseph; being put in an empty pit Gen. 37:24. And they took him, and cast him into a pit, and the pit was empty, there was no water in it.
6. Joseph; Sold by his brethren Gen. 37:28. Then there passed by Midianites merchantmen, and they drew and lifted up Joseph out of the pit, and sold Joseph to the Ishmaelites for twenty pieces of silver, and they brought Joseph into Egypt.
7. Joseph; Lifted up from the empty pit Gen. 37:28. They drew and lifted up Joseph out of the pit.

8. Joseph; His disappearance brought much astonishment Gen. 37:29. Reuben, his brother, returned unto the pit and, behold, Joseph was not in the pit, and he rent his clothes. And he returned unto his brethren, and said, The child is not; and I, whither shall I go?

9. Joseph; the exalted one in Egypt Gen. 41:14–57. Joseph brought out of prison and exalted in Egypt.

Do we know of one whose life fits the description of Joseph? Only our Lord Jesus Christ.

1. Jesus; The beloved of the Father Mathew chapter 3 vs 17, And lo a voice from heaven, saying This is my beloved Son, in whom I am well pleased.

2. Jesus; Hated by His brethren John 15:25. But this cometh to pass, that the word might be fulfilled that is written in their law. They hated me without a cause.

3. Jesus; Conspired against by his brethren Matt. 26:3–4. Then assembled together the chief priests, and the scribes, and the elders of the people, unto the palace of the high priest, who was called Caiaphas; and consulted that they might take Jesus by subtilty and kill him.

4. Jesus; stripped out of his coat Matt 27:28. And they stripped Him and put on him a scarlet robe

5. Jesus; Being put in an empty tomb Matt. 27:59–60. And when Joseph of Arimathaea had taken the body, he wrapped it in a clean linen cloth; And laid it in his own new tomb, which he had hewn out in the rock.

6. Jesus; Sold by His brethren. Matt. 26:14–15. Then one of the twelve, called Judas Iscariot, went unto the chief priests; And said unto them, What will ye give me, and I will deliver him unto you? And they covenanted with him for thirty pieces of silver.

7. Jesus; Lifted up from that empty tomb Acts 2:32. This Jesus hath God raised up whereof we all are witnesses.

8. Jesus; Disappearance brought about astonishment Matt; 28:5–6, 11–13, Luke 24:13–24; John 20:1–2.

9. Jesus; The Exalted one Acts 2:33. Therefore being by the right hand of God exalted, and having received of the Father the promise of the Holy Ghost he hath shed forth this which now see and hear. Therefore let all the house of Israel know assuredly, that God hath made that same Jesus, whom you have crucified, both Lord and Christ. The songwriter said:

> *"Man of Sorrow" what a name,*
> *For the Son of God who came;*
> *Ruined sinners to reclaim!*
> *Hal-le-lu-jah! what a Savior!*
>
> *Bearing shame and scoffing rude,*
> *In my place condemned He stood;*
> *Sealed my pardon with His blood;*
> *Hal-le-lu-jah! what a Savior!*

Hymns of Worship and Remembrance#96
Published by Gospel Perpetuating Publishers,
Fort Dodge, Iowa 50501

Notes:

77 – The Longsuffering of God

Luke 13:1–9

The chapter begins with the words: There were present at that season some that told him of the Galilaeans, whose blood Pilate had mingled with their sacrifices. Verse 2: And Jesus answering said unto them, Suppose ye that these Galilaeans were sinners above all the Galilaeans because they suffered such things? Verse 3: I tell you Nay; but except ye repent, ye shall all likewise perish.

Sometimes people make assessment on the holiness of others by what they know that may have happened to them. One is a sinner not by what happens to him, but by who he is as a result of Adam's transgressions. Romans 5:12 tells us, "Wherefore, as by one man sin entered into the world, and death by sin, and so death passed upon all men, for that all have sinned. Also in Romans we read; all have sinned and come short of the glory of God. Therefore in Luke 13:5 Jesus said, again, I tell you Nay: but except ye repent, ye shall all likewise perish.

According to the parable, we see:

1. The preparation for the fruit by the man, Luke 13 vs.6. He planted, he did what was necessary. Christ did all that was necessary and required that we should bear fruits of repentance, he went to the cross and died for our sins.
2. The expectation of the fruit by the man Luke 13 vs. 6. He came and sought fruit from the tree. If he did not do what was necessary he would not be looking for the fruit. After Christ has done everything that would meet the requirement for fruit bearing by us, it is reasonable to think that Christ would look for repentance from mankind. In Isaiah 5:1–2 we read of Israel, Jehovah's vineyard, how God was looking for fruits of repentance from them after he did all that was necessary, and how disappointing it was.

Now will I sing to my well-beloved a song of my beloved touching his vineyard. My well-beloved hath vineyard in very fruitful hill vs. 2; and he fenced it, and gathered out the stones thereof, and planted it with the choicest vine, and built a tower in the midst of it, and also made a winepress therein, and he looked that it should bring forth grapes, and it brought forth wild grapes. Vs. 3 and now, O inhabitants of Jerusalem, and men of Judah, judge, I pray you, betwixt me and my vineyard. Vs. 4; the big question, what could have been done more to my vineyard, that I have not done in it? Wherefore, when I looked that it should bring forth grapes, brought it forth wild grapes?

3. The destruction of the tree commanded by the man. Luke 13 vs. 7. The destruction was only commanded after a waiting period, and according to my background and experiences, with fruit from a fig tree, some places we call it a banana tree, three years was a long period. Therefore this verse speaks of the longsuffering of God as He is waiting for repentance. Is that from you? However, we also see the grace of God as He waits.

4. Extension of time requested by the dresser Luke 13 vs.8, showing a period of grace. Let it alone this year also, till I shall dig about, and dung it. Verse 9 says, and if it bear fruit, well: and if not then after that thou shall cut it down. This story is very meaningful to me, according to my testimony on page 45 in my book, *The Autobiography of Joseph Jeremiah*. God gives people time to repent. Hezekiah had fifteen more years Isaiah 38:1–5, but the rich man in Luke 12:16–20 did not have any more time. Our advice today is in 2 Cor. 6:2. Behold now is the accepted time, behold now is the day of salvation.

Notes:

78 – The Identity and Responsibility of the Believer in View of God's Judgment

1 Thess. 5:1–11

The Apostle Paul and Barnabas commended to the work of the Lord by the local church at Antioch in Syria, went from Antioch in Syria to Antioch in Pisidia up in Asia Minor. Notice how someone is commended or ordained by the local church to the work of the Lord for the glory of God Acts 13:1–46: (1) They were members of the local church where they and others were ministering; (2) the Holy Ghost said to the church, separate me Barnabas and Saul for the work where unto I have called them, this calling was to them personally with instruction to the local church; (3) they were sent forth by the Holy Spirit and recognized by the church; and (4) they identified by the church by the laying of hands on them and commending them to the work of the Lord.

Now therefore, the question can be asked: how are missionaries or workers sent out, commended, or ordained to full-time service in the work of the Lord? The answer is by the Holy Ghost; the individual must feel the calling of God on his life, and the Church must be spiritual to recognize that calling. Then the church should not refuse to commend that individual to the work of the Lord. Nothing is said there of salary; the going is by faith according to Phil. 4:19: but my God shall supply all your need according this riches in glory by Christ Jesus.

However it must be understood that everyone must eat, and God gives instructions on this also according to 1 Cor. 9:13–14 and Romans 15:27. It hath please them verily; and their debtors they are. For if the Gentiles have been made partakers of their spiritual things, their duty is also to minster unto them, (those who ministered), in carnal things. Carnal does not always referred to worldly or lack of spirituality, but literal things, such as bread, milk, money, and so forth. Therefore the preacher must be supported, by the local church and other Christians.

When God's work is done God's way, there is the assurance of His blessing as we can see their ministries in Asia and Europe, It is said that within one month, the Thessalonians had received all the great doctrines of the Christian faith: the doctrines of sin, salvation, assurance, anticipation, and the judgment of God. They knew of the church age and beyond. Having left Thessalonica, the Apostle went to Berea, Athens and then to Corinth in Greece where he wrote this epistle about AD 54.

Now in chapter 5 the apostle wrote: But of the times and seasons brethren ye have no need that I write unto you, because they were knowledgeable of the model walk of the believer. In verse 11 Paul reminded them of their Identity, Ye are the children of light, we are not of the night, nor of darkness. Paul reminded them that there are two classes of people in the world, those in the light and those in darkness. If we were all in darkness since we have been born according to Rom. 5:12, how did the change came that some are now in the light and some in darkness. It is being explained in 2 Cor. 4:6 which we studied in another outline.

To those of us who have responded to the call of God unto salvation, much exhortations are given as to our walk, but strong words are also given regarding the Day of the Lord. What is the Day of the Lord? When will such a day appear, and who will experience such a day? First, who will not experience such a Day? The believer who has accepted Christ as Savior will not be there, for those in the church of our Lord Jesus Christ will be gone at the rapture 1 Thess. 4:13–16, but those who have failed to trust Christ as savior in their lifetime and are still on this earth will experience the most undesirable and painful days yet to come, known as the Day of the Lord. See Dan 9:24–27, cf. Matt. 224:29–30, Rev. 19:11–21.

In view of this, what are our responsibilities? See 1 Thessalonian chapter 5 vs. 6–11, and may we be conscious of our identity and seek to carry out our responsibility while God is keeping us here.

Notes:

79 – Revelations on the Resurrection of Christ

John 20:1–31

The end of chapter 19 presents the record of the burial of our Lord Jesus Christ. Joseph of Arimathaea, a secret disciple, begged for the body of Christ, and Nicodemus another secret disciple brought 100 pounds of myrrh and aloes for the burial of Jesus Christ (Nicodemus seemed to have been a strong man to carry 100 pounds of myrrh.) What a fellowship and what devotion at the burial of Jesus Christ.

Now in chapter 20 we learn of the amazing discoveries at the resurrection of Jesus Christ. In Matt. 16:21, Jesus had said he must go to Jerusalem, suffer many things, be killed and be raised again the third day. With this we see:

1. The discovery of the women who saw how he was buried Matt. 28:1, Mark 16:1–6, Luke 24:1–10, John 20:1. The open tomb vs. 1–2.
2. The discovery of the other disciple, who did outrun Peter John 20 vs. 3–5
3. The discovery of Peter who went into the sepulcher and the napkin wrapped together in a place by itself John 20 vs. 6–7.
4. The discovery of Mary who stayed by the sepulcher; two angels and Jesus himself John 20 vs. 11–16.
5. The departure of Jesus to the Father and our God John 20 vs. 17. The hymn writer said:

> *There in righteousness transcendent;*
> *Lo! He doth in heaven appear,*
> *Shows the blood of His atonement;*
> *As thy tittle to be there.*

The work is done; Jesus reported back to the Father who sent him.

All thy sins were laid upon Him,
Jesus bore them on the tree;
God, who knew them, laid them on Him,
And, believe thou are free.
Hymns of Worship and Remembrance#120
J Denham Smith 1817-1889

6. The delighted disciples: Then the same day at evening being the first day of the week, when the doors were shut where the disciples were assembled for fear of the Jews, came Jesus and stood in the midst, and said unto them: "Peace be unto you" and then shewed them His hands and His side. Then were the disciples glad when they saw the LordJohn 20 vs. 19–20.

7. The declaration of the Holy Spirit: In John 16:7 Jesus said, The coming of the Holy Spirit, the Comforter, will be as he. Jesus ascends up to heaven fifty days after his death. Therefore after he had said "Peace be unto you," He breathed on them, and said unto them Receive ye the Holy Ghost, that is the one whom he previously said will be in them, the declaration was made but the manifestation will be on the Day of Pentecost Acts 2:1

8. The doubtful Thomas now present John 20 vs. 24–29. Jesus appeared in eight days, and Thomas was there. Jesus showed His hands and his sides for certification that it was he who was crucified, but raised from the dead. Thomas would not be deprived of the glorious sight. Thomas would not be left out from the company of the disciples, for he was in fellowship all the time, and now he would not be left out. There we see Jesus not only revealed himself to Thomas but as the Author of unity among brethren.

9. The divine purpose of these revelations John 20 vs.30- 31. But these are written that ye might believe that Jesus is the Christ the Son of God; and that believing ye might have life through his name.

Notes:

80 – *Thanksgiving Celebration for church Dedications*
Neh. 12:2, 31–32, 38–43

The end of Israel's seventy years in captivity and the end of the Babylonian Empire resulted in the Medo-Persian Empire, under the leadership of Cyrus king of Persia and Darius king of Medes. For background on the events leading up to this action by Cyrus king of Persia, we can recall the ten tribes of Israel who were disobedient to God, taken into captivity in Assyria by King Hoshea, and were placed in Halah and in Habor by the river Gozan, and in the cities of the Medes 2 Kings 17:6–18. Then the two tribes Judah and Benjamin by not listening to the prophets Isaiah and Jeremiah were taken into captivity in Babylon by King Nebuchadnezzar. It's one thing to be disobedient, but it's another thing to experience the consequences. In Psalm 137 we read, by the rivers of Babylon we sat down, yea, we wept, when we remembered Zion, or how they were before.

Now at the end of the Babylonian Empire, Cyrus king of Persia made a proclamation that Israel can return to Jerusalem and rebuild the temple. That expedition was led by Zerubbabel, so many of both captivities went back, but some did not feel the need to return. Later Ezra returned and established worship, and about fourteen years later, that is, about 444 BC, Nehemiah went up and built the walls. The temple took 7seven years to be built Ezra 6:15, and the wall took fifty-two days to be built Neh. 6:15. Now it was time for the dedication of the wall:

1. The people who led the thanksgiving: The Levites, or those of the priestly line Neh. 12:27. We as believers are a Royal Priesthood, a holy nation 1 Peter 2:9.
2. The purpose of the thanksgiving: To keep the dedication with gladness Nehemiah 12 vs. 27b, according to reflection as to where they came from and now it's a landmark. We too can have a backward look and say, Hitherto hath the Lord helped us.

3. The program for the thanksgiving. With thanksgiving and singing Nehemiah 12:27c. Should we have the opportunity to dedicate a building for which the Lord has given us, this is an example. But also we should be giving thanks to God for having delivered us from the power of darkness into His marvelous light.

4. The place of the thanksgiving: By the wall, right where it happened Nehemiah12 vs. 31. They did not go to some fancy place, like we might like to be at a five-star hotel, right where the Lord gave His blessing.

5. The pleasure in the thanksgiving Nehemiah 12 vs. 43. The whole assembly rejoiced, not a few brethren, but all members of the family.

6. The proclamation at the dedication Nehemiah 12 vs. 43b. The joy of Jerusalem was heard even afar off. No one complained of the noise, but the public got to know something was happening. This would draw attention to the nations around.

Notes:

CHAPTER 9

81 – The Life and Works of Jacob and His Return to God

The stolen birthright, the stolen blessing
Genesis 25:27–34, 27:1–33:

Esau his brother came from the field very hungry while Jacob was cooking. Esau said to Jacob, Feed me I pray thee with that same red pottage, for I am faint, therefore was his name called Edom. Jacob would feed him under one condition that Esau sell him his birthright, that which belongs to the firstborn in the family, for some pottage or today we might say some red beans. At the same time Esau did not see the importance of having his birthright, and Jacob seized the opportunity to get it from him. Also in Chapter 27 their father Isaac wanted savory meat from venison and requested it from Esau, and then he will bless him. But Jacob and his mother came up with a plan and stole the blessing which belongs to Esau. Jacob's name means supplanter, for he supplanted his brother by stealing his blessings.

The undesirable separation of Jacob Genesis 28:1–2

Isaac called Jacob and blessed him, and charged him, and said unto him. Thou shall not take a wife of the daughters of Canaan. Arise, go to Padan-aram, to the house of Bethuel thy mother's father, and take a wife from thence of the daughters of Laban thy mother's brother. And Isaac sent away Jacob; and he went to Padan-aram unto Laban, son of Bethuel, the Syrian, and the brother of Rebekah, Jacob's and Esau' mother vs. 5.

The personal conviction of Jacob vs. 10–14.

And Jacob went out from Beer-sheba, and went toward Haran. And he lighted upon a certain place, and tarried there all night. And he dreamed and behold a ladder set up on the earth, and the top of it reached to heaven: and behold the angels of God ascending and descending on it. And, behold the Lord stood above it, and said, I am the Lord God of Abraham thy father, and the God of Isaac: the land whereon thou liest to thee will I give it, and to thy seed.

In Genesis 28 Verse 15 and behold, I am with thee. And will keep the in all places whither thou goest, and will bring thee again into this land; for I will not leave thee, until I have done that which I have spoken to thee of. Vs.16 and Jacob awaked out of his sleep, and he said, Surely the Lord is in this place, and I knew it not. vs. 17 And Jacob rose up early in the morning and took the stone that he had. vs. 19 and he called the name of that place Bethel.

The Sincere Profession of Jacob Genesis 28 vs. 20–21: And Jacob vowed a vow, saying. If God will be with me, and will keep me in this way that I go, and will give me bread to eat, and raiment to put on, So that I come again to my father's house in peace, then shall the Lord be my God. Did the Lord keep Jacob in the way that he went? Yes, for God is faithful and keeps His promise forever. But did Jacob kept his promise according to his vow? No. After twenty years Jacob was returning, but instead of going Bethel according to his vow, he went to Shechem; he did not keep his vow to return to Bethel, the house of God, and by going to Shechem he was going downward in a backslidden direction from his fellowship with the Lord. By going there his daughter Dinah was defiled 34:1–2. His children had strange gods and earrings and so on. Things were going the wrong way. However, in 35:1—4 we read, God said unto Jacob. Arise, go up to Bethel and dwell there, and make there an altar unto God, that appeared unto thee when thou fleddest from the face of Esau thy brother. Then Jacob said unto his household and to all that were with him, Put away the strange gods that are among you, and be clean, and change your garments, and let us arise, and go up to Bethel; And they gave unto Jacob all the strange gods which were in their hand and all their earrings which were in their ears, and Jacob hid them under the oak which was by Shechem. With this we see:

The transgression of Jacob; he robbed his brother of his birthright and blessing. The conversion of Jacob: he met God at Bethel and made a commitment to worship and follow him. The misdirection of Jacob: he went in a backslidden state when he went to Shechem, but we see:

The complete restoration of Jacob; he responded to the call of God: *Arise, go up to Bethel and dwell there* Gen. 35:1.

Many reading this book might be in a backslidden state, but God is saying *Arise, go up to Bethel and dwell there*. Many call this revival, repentance, or just simply start reading the Bible and go back to church for restoration. *Arise, go up to Bethel and dwell there.*

Notes:

82 – The Person and Work of the Holy Spirit
John 14:16–17, Heb. 9:14, Acts 2:14

As we study the subject on the person and work of the Holy Spirit in light of God's word, we can see the Holy Spirit as the third person of the Godhead, being coexistant, coeternal and coequal with God; we can consider such passages as Deut. 33:27 where Moses blessing the children of Israel, to the tribe of Asher he said, "The eternal God is thy refuge and underneath are the everlasting arms." John 1:1 and 14 say, Jesus said of himself: In the beginning was the Word, and the Word was with God and the Word was God. And the Word was made flesh and dwelt among us. In Heb. 9:14 we read: How much more shall the blood of Christ, who through the eternal Spirit offered himself without spot to God. Then in Genesis 1:26, God said Let us make man, us being plural, included the three persons of the Godhead, Father, Son and Holy Spirit.

Now therefore, having seen the person of the Holy Spirit, we can consider the work of the Holy Spirit.

1. The promise of the Holy Spirit Joel 2:28. God said; And it shall come to pass afterward, that I will pour out my spirit upon all flesh, and this was fulfilled on the Day of Pentecost at the beginning of the church age. In Acts 2:17, Peter quoted Joel 2:28. Jesus said in John 14:16 And I will pray the Father, and he shall give you another Comforter, that he may abide with you forever. Again Jesus said in John 16:7, Nevertheless I tell you the truth, It is expedient for you that I go away, for if I go not away, the Comforter will not come unto you, but if I depart, I will send him unto you.

2. The presence of the Holy Spirit Acts 1:4. And being assembled together with them, commanded them that they should not depart from Jerusalem, but wait for the promise of the Father which saith he, ye have heard of me. Verse 8 says, But ye shall receive power, after that

the Holy Ghost is come upon you, and ye shall be witnesses unto me both in Jerusalem, and in all Judaea, and in Samaria, and unto the uttermost part of the earth. Acts 2:1 states, when the day of Pentecost was fully come, they were all with one accord in one place. Then to the end of the chapter we see the presence of the Holy Spirit.

3. The power of the Holy Spirit Acts 2:4. And they were all filled with the Holy Ghost, and began to speak with other tongues or languages, for there were fifteen different languages present there at Jerusalem. Verse 7 And they were all amazed and marvelled, saying one to another, Behold, are not all these which speak Galilaeans? Verse 8 And how hear we every man in our own tongue, wherein we were born? And what they heard were identified as the wonderful works of God.

4. The Possession of the Holy Spirit John 14:17. Jesus said but ye know him for He dwelleth with you and shall be in you. Romans 8:9 says, Now if any man have not the Spirit of Christ, he is none of His. Therefore, that one be qualified to be a child of God he must be indwelt by the Holy Spirit, which comes at the time of conversion. We do not tarry to receive the Holy Spirit, less it will be something we will be doing to have Him, but he comes at the time of conversions 1 Peter 1:2. That we be used by the Holy Spirit is that the Holy Spirit have more of us, and this is by living a life of holiness and practical sanctification to God. For by one Spirit are we all baptized into the body of Christ 1Cor. 12:13.

Notes:

83 – The Difference between the Law and the Grace of Our Lord Jesus Christ

Romans 8:1–17

There is therefore now no condemnation to them which are in Christ Jesus who walk not after the flesh, but after the Spirit. For the law of the Spirit of life in Christ Jesus hath made me free from the law of sin and death. For what the law could not do, in that it was weak through the flesh, God sent his own son in the likeness of sinful flesh, and for sin condemned sin in the flesh. That the righteousness of the law might be fulfilled in us, who walk not after the flesh, but after the Spirit.

These verses are there to explain what was said in Romans chapter 7:15–25 which speaks of the strife between two natures under the law. What I would, that I do not, but what I hate that I do. Then in vs. 24–25 Paul said, O wretched man that I am, who shall deliver me from the body of this death. I thank God that through Jesus Christ our Lord, So then with the mind I myself serve the law of God, but with the flesh the law of sin.

Whereas we see a life under the law was weak as man had limited victory. With the law of the spirit of life in Christ Jesus, man through faith in him has a greater victory over sin, that the apostle can say in 1 Corinthians 15:57 "Thanks be to God which giveth us the victory through our Lord Jesus Christ."

Notes:

84 – To Whom Belongest Thou?

1 Sam. 27:1–6, 28:1–2, 29:1–7, 30:1, 8–17

To whom belongest thou, and whence art thou

1 Samuel 30:13

The story surrounding these questions began from chapter 26, where we find that as king Saul was pursuing after David, he and his men could have been killed by David, but David would not touch the Lord's anointed and spared the life of Saul, Israel's first king. (David had respect for whom the Lord allowed to rule, and we should also.)

In chapter 27 David said in his heart, "I shall now perish one day by the hand of Saul, so he went and joined himself to Achish the king of Gath, who gave him a little inland town name Ziklag. In course of time, war broke out between Israel and the Philistines among whom David was living; this means David was in the enemy territory to Israel, but he, having an alliance with the king decided to join Achish the king of Gath with his 600 men to fight against Israel.

In 28:1–2 Ackish said unto David. Know thou assuredly, that thou shall go out with me to battle, thou and thy men. And David said to Ackish, surely thou shall know what thy servant can do.

In 29 1–7 is, now the Philistines gathered together all their armies to Aphek and the Israelites pitched by a fountain which is in Jezreel. The princes of the Philistines said unto Achish the king; Make this fellow return, that is to send David to his little town Ziklag, the king did not want to do that knowing how powerful David was with his 600 men, but as the princes or his generals pressed upon him, he asked David to return to his little town Ziklag.

In 30:1–8 we read: And it came to pass, that when David and his men were come to Ziklag on the third day, that the Amalekites had invaded the south, and Ziklag, and smitten Ziklag, and burned it with fire. They also had taken the women whom David and his men had left in the city and carried them away. So David and his men came to the city, and behold it was burned with fire, and their wives, and their sons and their daughters were taken captives, including David two wives. David was greatly distressed, for the people spake of stoning him. What do we do when everyone is against us? What did David do? He encouraged himself in the Lord, and sought guidance from the Lord, (an example for us according to Hebrews 13:5) God gave him the green light to go after his enemies.

Now is our message according to topic. As they were pursuing the Amalekites (30:11–17), they found an Egyptian in the field, and brought him to David: They gave him bread, and he did eat, they made him drink water, a piece of a cake of figs, and two clusters of raisins. And when he had eaten, his spirit came again to him, for he had eaten no bread, nor drunk any water, three days and three nights. This man got water, appetizer, the main course and dessert, so now he had strength to answer questions.

Question number 1 1st Samuel 30 vs. 13: To whom belongest thou?

Question number 2 whence are thou. Vs. 13. The man gave the true answers; I am a young man of Egypt, servant to an Amalekite, and my master left me, because three days ago I fell sick. Vs. 14; We made an invasion upon the South of the Cherethites, and upon the course which belongeth to Judah, and upon the south of Caleb, and we burned Ziklag with fire.

Now therefore we see:

1. The condition of the man 1st Samuel 30 vs. 11–12. Sick and helpless and ready to die.
2. The provision for the man. A three course meal, he got dessert too vs. 11–12
3. The identification of the man vs. 13. He said who he was.
4. The confession of the man vs. 14. He said what he and his associates did.

5. The adoption of the man vs. 15–16. He was taken by David and company.

6. The protection of the man vs. 15–16. Should the enemy try to do him harm, that enemy must first defeat David and his men. The man did not have to protect himself; he now had protection.

Application: As we consider our relationship with God, we see ourselves spiritually in the same condition as the man and share the same blessings as he had.

Egypt is a type of living the worldly life of sin and separation from God.

Amalek is a type of the flesh, everything for self without considering God.

1. The condition of man before God. Man is sick with sin and ready to die in that condition Romans 3:10–18, cf. Isaiah. 1:4–6.

2. The provision for man. All by God's love to man John 3:16, Rom. 5:8.

3. The identification of man according to scriptures Rom. 3:23.

4. The confession of man as he sees his need of a Savior Rom. 10:9–10.

5. The adoption of man by God John 1:12, Gal. 3:26, 4:4–6.

6. The protection of man by God John 10:27–28, Jude. 1, 1 Peter2:5.

Notes:

85 – The Person and Work of Christ as Seen in the Psalms and Revealed in the New Testament

There are sixteen psalms prophetically providing information on the person and work of Christ. We would like to look at six of these psalms relating to the work of Christ for our salvation and his high priestly office.

In Luke 24:25–27 we read: And certain of them which were with us went to the sepulchre, and found it even so as the women had said, but him they saw not. Then he said unto them, O fools and slow of heart to believe all that the prophets have spoken. Ought not Christ to have suffered these things, and to enter into his glory? And beginning at Moses and all he prophets, he expounded unto them in all the scriptures the things concerning himself. Therefore, of the six Psalms we see *Old Testament* and *New Testament*

1. The Incarnation of Christ Psalm 40:6–7 Heb. 10:6–7
2. The Temptation of Christ Psalm 91:1–11; Matt. 4:1–11.
3. The Betrayal of Christ Psalm 41:9; Matt. 26:14–16, John 13:21–27.
4. The Crucifixion of Christ Psalm 22:7–18; Matt. 27:33–35.
5. The resurrection of Christ Psalm 16:10; Matt. 28:1–6.
6. Ascension of Christ Psalm 68:18; Acts 1:8–9.

Notes:

86 – The Saddest Time in the Life of Israel

1st Sam. 2:12–17, 27–36 and chapter 4 : 1-22.

It is said that God buries his workmen, but his work goes on; the burials are either by old age, illness, or disobedience. The story in these chapters do not indicate the many deaths were by old age or illness, but rather as a result of the sins committed by Hophni and Phinehas, the sons of Eli the priest of the Lord. With this we see:

1. The privilege of Hophni and Phinehas: They were from the priestly line, from the tribe of Levi; they knew what was required and expected of them.

2. The practice of Hophni and Phinehas: They were committing serious immoral acts with the children of Israel while partaking in the things which belong to the priests living holy lives 1ˢᵗ Samuel 2:12–17.

3. The prophecy of the man of God 2:27–34. He first reminded Eli of God's mercy and faithfulness to Israel, their deliverance from bondage in Egypt, their safekeeping over the years, and what God expected of them, but they failed. Then he spoke to them of the judgment that would fall upon them due to the lifestyles of Hophni and Phinehas— they both would die in one day vs. 34.

4. The promise of a change in priestly activities 2:35–36. God said, I will raise me up a faithful priest that shall do according to that which is in my heart and mind, and will build him a sure house; and he shall walk before mine anointed forever. And it shall come to pass, that every one that is left in thine house shall come and crouch to him for a peace of silver and a morsel of bread, and shall say, Put me, I pray thee unto one of the priests offices, that I may eat a piece of bread.

    The faithful priest mentioned is referred to by William McDonald as Zadok of the house of Eleazar who ministered in the days of David and Solomon, but many see a messianic allusion in the faithful priest of verse 35, partly in light of the word *forever*.

5. The preparation for battle with the Philistines 4:1–5. Israel went out against the Philistines to battle. They were smitten before the Philistines, and wandered why, so the thought of a plan that they might be victorious, they said, Let us fetch the ark of the covenant of the Lord out of Shiloh unto us, that when it cometh among us it may save us out of the hand of our enemies. What a mistake? In vs. 10–11 we are told, the Ark or God was taken and the two sons of Eli Hophni and Phinehas were slain. Moreover, the wife of Phinehas was about to deliver a child, when she got the bad news that the Ark of God was taken, her husband, brother-in law and father-in law were dead, she bowed herself and travailed, and as she was about to die, she named her son that was born, Ichabod, meaning, The glory is departed from Israel, because the ark of God was taken and because her father in law, her brother-in law, and her husband were all killed in the battle. What a sad day in the life of Israel. The glory is departed.

Application: Sometimes people ask the question. Why do bad things happen to good people? The answer is bad things happen to anyone; sometimes it is for testing, like Job, and sometimes it is because of sin. For while God is the God of all grace, he is also a God of righteousness and can by no means spare the guilty.

Notes:

87 – The Suffering of Christ and the Glory that has followed 1st Peter 1:1–11.

As we consider this passage in light of the sovereign grace of God, we can think of ourselves as having nothing to do in the plan and program of God, but only our acceptance of such a plan and program. While we generally consider a passage from its beginning, I would like us to consider this passage from the last verse in this study—verse 11. This verse presents the core of God's plan of salvation by the suffering of Christ, the abundant life to be realized by the children of God, and the glory that would follow.

These words were spoken by the prophets because of the Spirit of Christ which was in them, or moved upon them, such as Isaiah 53:5. He was wounded for our transgressions. But someone will say or ask a question: Did not the Holy Spirit come on the Day of Pentecost? Take note that in the Old Testament, the Holy Spirit came upon prophets at certain times and to accomplish certain missions, but in the New Testament, according to the promise of Christ, that upon acceptance of Him as Savior and Lord the Holy Spirit will come and make His abode in the believer and will abide with him forever with manifestations such as those recorded in John 16:7–15, which began from the Day of Pentecost Acts chapter 2. And the ministry will continue to the time in 2 Thess. chapter 2.

In Matt. 16:21 after Jesus spoke of the church He would build, he said he must go to Jerusalem, suffer many things, be killed, and be raised up the third day. In Matt.21 Jesus went to Jerusalem, and then in Matt. 27:33–35, Jesus was killed, but there were seven cries Jesus made on the cross:

1. My God, My God why has Thou forsaken me Matt. 27:46, Mark 15:34. The songwriter said, "Scorned by man by God forsaken."
2. Father forgive them for they know not what they do Luke 23:34. The compassionate Christ.

3. Today shall thou be with me in paradise Luke 23:43. The consolation of Christ.

4. Father into thy hand I commit my spirit Luke 23:46. Not my will but Thine be done.

5. Woman behold thy son John 19:26. What a sight His earthly mother had to see her son suffering as no man suffered.

6. I thirst John 19:28. A parched tongue; and

7. It is finished John 19:30. The work required for our salvation was done; Christ died for our sins according to the scriptures 1 Cor. 15:1–3.

Now for the glory which followed, we see:

1. The glory of his resurrection Matt. 28:1–6, Acts 2:24; Never in the history of mankind has such a thing happened 1 Cor. 15:20.

2. The glory by his exaltation Acts 2:33

3. The glory of his intercession Heb. 9:24

4. The glory by our approach to a holy God, in contrast to Israel Lev. 16, cf. 2 Cor. 3:7–12. The songwriter said, "Why stand we then without in fear, the blood of Christ invites us near."

5. The glory of our inheritance: wisdom, knowledge, the present enjoyment and the future hope of the believer.

6. The glory that shall be revealed Romans 8:18, 1 Peter 1:9. Receiving the end of your faith, even the salvation of your souls (at the rapture, 1 Thess. 4:13–16).

7. The glory of the salvation that is past, present, and future—2 1:10: Who delivered us from so great a death (past) who doth deliver us (present), in whom we trust that he will yet deliver us (future).

Notes:

88 – The Superiority of Christ

Matt. 12:38–41

The definition of superiority: higher in position, higher in rank, higher in authority. Now we see:

The superiority of Christ in relation to Jonah Matt. 12:38–41

What made Jonah great was his obedience to God's call to him to preach at Nineveh, the impending judgment of God coming their way, and the city saved by the obedience of Jonah Jonah 3:1–10. And though Jonah was great by this act, Jesus said He was greater than Jonah.

The superiority of Christ in relation to Solomon Matt. 12:42

What made Solomon great was his wisdom and judgment. An example is recorded in 1 King 3:16–28 regarding two women who came to him about their babies that were born and their dispute over whose child was dead, whose child was living, and who should get the living child. Also, and example is in 4:29–34 how God gave to Solomon wisdom and understanding exceeding much, and largeness of heart, even as the sand that is on the seashore. The visit by the Queen of Sheba and her remarks, that the half has not been told her as to who this man was 10:1–7.

The superiority of Christ in relation to the prophets Heb. 1:1–2.

The greatness of Christ is seen in his deity Heb. 1:1–9, 2:5–8.

The greatness of Christ is seen in his words Matt. 7:2; 8–29.

The greatness of Christ is seen in his love John 15:13, John 10:17–18.

The greatness of Christ is seen in his salvation Heb. 2:1–3. All of these and more present to us the superiority of Christ.

Notes:

89 – The Sweet and Bitter Story on the Life of Sampson
Judges–16 Verses 1-31

The children of Israel was led by Moses the servant of God from Egypt Exodus 12:1 to the land of Moab Deuteronomy 34:5–12. And then by Joshua, Moses' minister from Moab to the land of Canaan Joshua 1:1–24:33. After the death of Joshua they were ruled by thirteen judges for about 450 years, of whom Samson was the last Acts 13:20. The key verse in the book of Judges is chapter 17 verse 6: "In those days there was no king in Israel, but every man did that which was right in his own eyes", and the Lord delivered them into the hands of the Philistines forty years, but He raised up a man named Samson to be their deliverer.

As we study the sweet and bitter story of Samson's life we see:

1. The divine providence at the birth of Samson Judges 13:2–5: For lo, thou shall conceive, and bear a son, and no razor shall come on his head; for the child shall be a Nazarite unto God from the womb. And he shall begin to deliver Israel out of the hand of the Philistines. The child shall be a Nazarite, (one separated unto God.) from the womb: and he shall begin to deliver Israel out of the hand of the Philistines, then Manoah his father said; Now let thy words come to pass. How shall we order the child, and how shall we do unto him? We do not need to ask this question today because it is in God's word. Proverbs 22:6 says Train up a child in the way he should go, and when he is old he will not depart from it.

2. The divine grace in the life of Samson Judges 13:24–25. The Spirit of the Lord began moving in the life of Samson.

3. The downward path and disgrace to God by Samson Judges 14:1–7. Samson went down to Timnath and saw a woman in Timnath of the daughters of the Philistines. And he came up, and told his father and his mother, and said I have seen a woman in Timnath of the daughters

of the Philistines, now therefore get her for me to wife. Then his father and his mother said unto him. Is there never a woman among the daughters of thy brethren, or among all my people that thou goest to take a wife of the uncircumcised Philistines: And Samson said unto his father Get her for me; for she pleaseth me well. (This is a picture of a believer getting married to an unbeliever.)

4. The disclosure of the secret of Samson's strength Judges 14:18–16:20. Samson having been lowered, gave away the secret of his strength. But now he thought he was the same and could go out in his strength as before, but the Lord had departed from him 16:20.

    Application: When a person receives Christ as savior and received the Holy Spirit in his life, he can do great things for God, but if he lives a sinful life and misses the fellowship with God, he is still in the right relationship with God, but out of fellowship with God and can run into serious problems both physical and spiritual. The sad part is that he thinks he is the same as Samson. He did not know that the Lord was departed from him. Therefore, the exhortation is: Grieve not the Holy Spirit Ephesians 4:30. Quench not the Holy Spirit 1 Thess. 5:19

Notes:

90 – The Three Big Questions in Matthew 24:1–14

*I*n Matthew 24:1–14 we read, "And Jesus went out and departed from the temple, and His disciples came to him for to shew him he buildings of the temple. And Jesus said unto them, See ye not all these things? Verily I say unto you, there shall not be left here one stone upon another that shall not be thrown down.

And as he sat upon the Mount of Olives, the disciples came unto him privately saying, Tell us (1) When shall these things be? Or When shall no stone be left upon another; (2) and what shall be the sign of thy coming, or what should we be looking for to know that Thy coming is near; and (3) The end of the world, or How the end of the world will be. These are very important questions deserving our attention;

In answer to the questions, Jesus gave a list of events that will happen:

(a) The destruction of the temple Matt 24: vs. 2.

(b) The deception of false teachers Matt 24.vs. 5.

(c) The declaration of wars Matt 24 vs. 6.

(d) The description of human suffering Matt 24 vs. 7–8.

(e) The disregard to human lives 2 vs. 8–13.

(f) The Gospel of the kingdom 24 vs. 14.

For all of the above, we see, as it were, a package according to Daniel 9:20–27 to include (1) The death of Christ, (2) postresurrection of Christ to the present time, and (3) events that will follow the rapture or the coming of Christ for his church.

In Daniel 9:20–27 we read that while Daniel was speaking and praying at Babylon, and God revealed to him seventy weeks of years when certain things will happen. The things to happen were broken down in three areas, each of which will be fulfilled according to God's purpose and timing: (1) the going forth from Babylon to rebuild Jerusalem; (2) the

Messiah (Christ) will be cut off but not for himself; and (3) the people of the prince shall destroy the city and the sanctuary.

The first was fulfilled at the end of the Babylonian Empire to the Medo-Persian Empire when Cyrus the king made a proclamation that Israel could go back and rebuild Jerusalem and the temple. This was fulfilled when the returning remnant of 42,360 besides their servants, maids, singing men, and singing women, totaling 49,697, went up with Zerubbabel Ezra 2:2–65. Later Ezra and Nehemiah went up, established worship, and built the wall.

The second was fulfilled when Messiah was cut off but not for himself, that is, when Jesus died on the cross Isaiah 53:8; Matt 27:51. Jesus did not have a sickbed; he was arrested as it were on Thursday, and he was dead by Friday. His death was not for himself; if not then for whom? For the ungodly, for you and me. Then as we accept Christ as Savior, we then become children of God and candidates for heaven Galatians 3:26.

In Matt. 24 Jesus did not mentioned his death, but the destruction of the city and the sanctuary or Temple to be fulfilled in AD 70, but Messiah must first be cut off or died for our sins, after which we see the events as stated previously happens and continue even to the days in which we are living. Then all will be fulfilled when the gospel of the kingdom will again be preached during the tribulation unto the revelation of Christ, when He comes to the earth in fulfillment of God's covenant with David that one will be on his throne.

Notes:

CHAPTER 10

91 – Tips on Door-to-Door Witnessing

1. Try to go by twos, with one speaking partner at a time, and one silent partner at a time. The silent partner's job is to control distractions or speak a word at the appropriate time.

2. When going to a home, try to be quiet, no loud talking or even singing; this may allow the dog to take its rest, and may avoid the resident from putting the chain on the door.

3. After you have knocked on the main door, step back behind the screen door and wait about one minute, if no answer, knock the door the second time, and if no answer leave a package of gospel literature, maybe on the doorknob. Under no circumstances you should put anything in a person's mailbox, someone may come after you and put something in also, and it could be something strange, or frightful to the resident.

4. The speaking partner responsibilities. If residents show interest in your visit or invite you to come in, use wisdom and do not be critical of their home; instead say a complimentary word, such as your lawn looks very good—that is, if it looks good—otherwise say nothing. Be wise and look with wisdom, not gazing through the house because they may observe you, be suspicious, and think you have other objectives than sharing the gospel with them. We are not in the 1940s; we are in the 21st century.

   However, look around to see if there are children's toys, bicycles, and so on, and then ask them if they have children for Sunday school. If they say yes, ask if they can bring them to your Sunday school, for if you get the children, you may get the parents also. If they invite you in as they are looking at TV, never stand in front of the TV to block their view. Instead, say, "Sorry to interrupt you." Most of the time they will turn off the TV.

5. The silent partner's responsibilities. If there are children that may prevent their parents from paying attention to the speaking partner, if the children seems to be friendly, try to take them apart from their parents, but don't force them. If is a boy or a girl and the silent partner is a female she may take anyone, but if the silent partner is a male, it is recommended that he only take a boy. These are things to keep out distractions so that the speaking partner can give the message.

6. When leaving the home, say nothing about your visit until you both have gone a few blocks from the home, the homeowner might be looking and may hear you saying something negative, which would ruin any chance you may have for a second visit. In everything always be in attitude of prayer, and always have 3 x 5 cards to take names and addresses to bring back for follow-ups.

Notes:

92 – We Pass This Way But Once

Heb. 9:27, Job 14:14, John 5:28, 1st Thess. 4:13–18, Rev. 20:5–6; 20:11–15
(Funeral)

Life is like a one-way street; we cannot go back and relive it all over again. The only thing we can do that is to take a backward look, consider our present with regard to our relationship to God, and make the necessary adjustments for a better future and blessing at our final destination. With this, we can look at a few scriptures that may help us in this regard.

1. We have an appointment with God Hebrews 9:27. For it is appointed unto men (all mankind) once to die, but after this the judgment. The appointment was not negotiated; we did not have any input into it. It was all done by a sovereign God.

2. We have a time of expectation regarding death Eccl. 3:2. A time to be born and a time to die. But Job ask the question in Job. 14:14: If a man die will he live again? Job recognized there is an appointed time to die, but does it mean that is all? No, Job said, all the days of my appointed time will I wait, till my change come.

3. We have a time of separation when that change comes John 5:28. Jesus said; Marvel not at this: for the hour is coming, in which all that are in the graves shall hear his voice; And shall come forth, they that have done good unto the resurrection of life, and they that have done evil, unto the resurrection of damnation. With this, we see there will be two resurrections; but how far apart would they be? According to God's timetable as seen in the scriptures, the time apart will be 1,007 years. The first resurrection is recorded in 1 Thessalonians 4:13–18, the ones mentioned there are those who have accepted the Bible as God's word to us; they believe in John 3:16. They have repented of their sins, they accepted Jesus Christ as Savior before they died physically, and

now Christ, according to His promise in John 14:1–3, has returned for them by coming in the clouds of heaven. In Revelation 20:5–6 we read, But he rest of the dead live not again until the thousand years were finished; This is the first resurrection. Blessed and holy is he that hath part in the first resurrection.

4. We have a time of condemnation, according to Rev. 20:11–15. This is at the second resurrection, and it will be only for those who did not receive Christ as their Savior during their lifetime here on earth. But the Lord is not willing that any should perish, but that all should come to repentance 2 Peter 3:9. That is why the message of the gospel is going out today—God's good news to a guilty world. Blessed and holy is he that hath part in the first resurrection. The question can be asked: which resurrection do you expect to be in—the first or the last? You can know today, or you should know today. For if you are saved and became a child of God Galatians 3:26, you are one in His church whom Christ will be coming for, and you are known as a believer, one of the brethren, a Christian, a disciple, a saint, and a soldier. But if not you are heading to a lost eternity. Read again John 5:28: all that are in the grave shall come forth. It's a matter of which group will you belong. The songwriter said:

> Sinners, whither will you wander?
> Whither will you stray?
> Oh, remember, life is slender,
> "Tis but a short day.
> Chorus:
> Death is coming, coming, coming;
> And the judgment day;
> Hasten sinner, hasten sinner,
> Seek the narrow way.

Redemption Song Book #242
Harper Collins Publishers,
77-85 Fulham Palace Road, London W6-8JB.

Notes:

93 – Why Wait Longer?
John 5:1–15

It is said; Opportunity knocks but once, but there are times you might miss an opportunity and be able to get caught up with it again. However, there is an opportunity for everyone that if missed, it's not possible to get caught up with again. In this story we see a man who was sick and was instantly healed.

In the gospel of John chapter 5 we read: There was a feast of the Jews, and Jesus went up to Jerusalem. Now there is at Jerusalem by the sheep market a pool with 5 porches or 5 entrances to get in. In these lay a great multitude of sick folks waiting for the moving of the water. For an angel went down at a certain season into the pool and troubled the water. Whosoever then first after the troubling of the water stepped in was made whole of whatsoever disease he had. And a certain man was there, which had an infirmity or disease for thirty eight years. But we can see:

1. The day of opportunity for the man John 5 vs. 1–5. The man was in the right place, at the right time, for the right purpose, he was there to be healed.

2. The evident disability of the man vs. 6. He was sick, lying in a bed, helpless, and ready to die. Jesus asked him one question: Wilt thou be made whole? Jesus knew of his condition, but the man must express his own desire.

3. The expression of sincerity by the man vs. 7. I have no man, or I would like to be healed, but I am helpless.

4. The instant and effective remedy for the man John 5 vs. 8–9. Jesus said, Rise, take up by bed and walk. The man was made whole the same time, not gradually, cf. 4:50–54.

5. The full and sincere loyalty of the man John 5 vs. 10–11. He was charged of breaking the Sabbath, but he was following orders from

the one who healed him. He said, "He that made me whole the same said unto me; Take up thy bed and walk."

6. The final and consistent activity of the man John 5 vs. 14. Jesus found him in the temple. Now he had an interest in the things of the Lord and was in the place where he could learn God's word.

Application: the Bible speaks of all mankind as being sick with sin Isaiah 1: vs 6

No one can heal himself or his brother; we are all sick helpless and ready to die. But there is the great physician, even Jesus who died for our sin, that we might be healed from our sin sick souls. Jesus is speaking to us by his Holy Spirit saying, Will thou be made whole? The man answered by himself, I have no one to help me. But praise God we do have someone to help us—Jesus Christ. Jesus gave a command, take thy bed and walk. In Hebrews 3:7–8 we read, today if ye will hear His voice, harden not your heart.

After the man was healed, he was found in the temple. If we trust in Christ for our salvation, where should be but in the local church where His word is spoken, and where we can learn how to live for him?

Notes:

94 – Women in the Bible who God used to accomplish His purposes
Rahab—Joshua chapters 1–2

After the death of Moses, the servant of the Lord, the Lord spake unto Joshua saying, Moses my servant is dead; Now therefore arise, go over his Jordan, thou and all this people unto the land which I do give to them, even to the children of Israel. (God assured Joshua that he will be with him); There shall not any man be able to stand before thee all the days of thy life: as I was with Moses, so I will be with thee: I will not fail thee, nor forsake thee Joshua 1:. 1–5.

Then Joshua commanded the officers of the people, saying, Pass through the host, and command the people, saying, Prepare ye victuals or food, for within three days ye shall pass over this Jordan, to go in to possess the land, which the Lord your God giveth you Joshua 1 vs. 10–11.

And Joshua the son of Nun sent out of Shittim two men to spy secretly, saying, Go view the land, even Jericho. And they went and came into an harlot's house, named Rahab, and lodged there. And it was told the king of Jericho saying Behold, there came men in tonight of the children of Israel to search out the country. And the king of Jericho sent unto Rahab, saying, Bring forth the men that are come to thee, which are entered into thine house, for they come to search out all the country Joshua 2:1–3.

The life and works of Rahab the harlot:

Rahab, the God-fearing harlot, expressed concerns for her city. And the woman took the two men and hid them, and said; there came men unto me, but I do not know from where they were. And it came to pass, about the time of shutting of the gate, when it was dark, that the men went out, where the men went I do not know. Go after them quickly, for you shall overtake them. But she had brought them up to the roof of the house, and hid them in order upon the roof. But before they were laid down, she came unto them upon the roof; and said unto the men. I know that the Lord hath given you the land, and that your terror is fallen upon us; for we have heard how the Lord dried up the water of the Red sea for you, when you came out of Egypt, and what you did to the two kings of the Amorites vs. 4–10.

Rahab sought security for herself and family: Now therefore, I pray you, swear unto me by the Lord, since I have shewed you kindness, that ye will also shew kindness unto my father's house, and give me a true token. And that you will save alive my father, and my mother, and my brethren, and my sisters, and all that they have and deliver our lives from death Joshua2: vs.12-13

Rahab received assurance of her safety: And the men said unto her; we will be blameless of this thine oath which thou hast made us swear. Behold, when we come into the land, thou shalt bind this line of scarlet thread in the window which thou didst let us down by. And she said; according unto your words, so be it. And she sent them away and they departed; then she bound the scarlet line in the window.

Now after this we have not read that Rahab remained in the same lifestyle as before her encounter with these men. Rather her name is listed in the genealogy of Jesus as recorded in Matthew 1:5 and in the hall of fame with the heroes of faith as recorded in Hebrews 11:31.

Application: God can use anyone to accomplish His purpose when that one turns to him in faith, fears him, and does his will. The lesson from this story is that it doesn't matter what our lifestyle may be, if we turn to God by faith, and in our case receive Christ as Savior, we too will be in the hall of fame or in the church of our Lord Jesus Christ, and God will use us to accomplish his purposes for His glory.

The spies returned to Joshua, Israel crossed Jordan unto the Promised Land, and destroyed the city of Jericho, all because Rahab the harlot feared God and allowed God to use her. At same time she and her family was secure and did not perish in the war because of the assurance the spies gave her as she put a red string in her window.

Notes:

95 – Women in the Bible Who God Used to Accomplish His Purposes

Naomi and Ruth—Ruth chapters 1–2

1. The departure of Naomi Ruth chapter 1:1–2. Now it came to pass in the days when the judges ruled, that there was a famine in the land, and a certain man of Bethlehem-Judah went to sojourn in the country of Moab, he and his wife and his two sons. We can think that their moving to the country of Moab was for economic reasons, as many do when things are hard in their country.

2. The discouragement of Naomi Ruth chapter 1:vs. 3-5 Noam lost her husband and her two her two sons , the bread winners passed away, leaving her with her two daughters-in-law, but she heard in the country of Moab how that the Lord had visited his people of Israel in giving them bread, so now we see.

3. The decision of Naomi because of good news chapter 1: vs 6–13. Naomi arose with her daughters-in-law to return to Bethlehem-Judah, so they went forth from the place they were to return, both Ruth and Orpah. Naomi would not force them to go with her; they must make their own decision. We can say of Orpah that she was inclined to go, and she made a step to go, but she made the wrong choice. She went back to her gods and to her people who worship idols. She could have been in an environment where she would have learned the things of God and have fellowship with those that know the love of God, but she failed and denied herself a wonderful opportunity to serve God and be blessed by Him.

4. The choice of Ruth—the true God Ruth 1:14–15. Ruth and Orpah lifted up their voices and wept, Orpah kissed her mother-in-law and returned to the land of Moab, but Ruth clave unto her. Naomi said, behold thy sister in law is gone back after thy sister-in-law. Again

Naomi would not force Ruth to come with her for this is a personal decision.

5. The commitment of Ruth—fully persuaded Ruth 1:16–22. Ruth said, intreat me not to leave thee, whether thou goest I will go, thy people shall be my people and thy God my God.

6. The contentment of Ruth—fully satisfied; Ruth 2:1–7. Ruth found employment with a rich man named Boaz who is a kinsman/redeemer to Naomi's husband Elimelech.

7. The caring of Ruth—fully appreciated Ruth 2:8–10. Boaz the kinsman/redeemer made provision for and gave protection to Ruth.

8. The comfort of Ruth—fully informed; Ruth 2:11–13. Boaz explained his knowledge of her and her step of faith in coming unto a people she did not know before, but all of the blessings came by her choice in the land of Moab. The blessings have extended to us by Jesus Christ, but the principle for blessings in Christ is on the principle of faith and our action of forsaking all else and choosing Christ. For in the genealogy of Christ in Matthew 1:5 we read: And Salmon begat Booz or Boaz and Booz begat Obed of Ruth, and Obed begat Jesse; and Jesse begat David the king.

Notes:

96 – Women in the Bible Who God Used to Accomplish His Purposes

Esther—chapters 1–10

It would be nice if everyone would read this story in the bible, especially our Jewish communities regarding the providence of God.

The key characters and events in the book of Esther can be seen as: Vashti put away, Esther chosen, Mordecai exalted, Haman hanged, and the feast of Purim instituted.

According to C. I. Scofield, "the name of God does not once occur, but in no other book of the Bible is His providence more conspicuous." We too cannot see a greater display of God's providence in the preservation of Israel from a holocaust that would have been unmatched to any we would know of in the history of mankind, for they were slated to be killed, every one, young and old, little children and women, in one day, even upon the thirteenth day of the twelfth month Esther 3:13. Now we will start with Vashti.

1. Vashti put away: Esther chapter 1: 1-22. Vashti was the first lady to Ahasuerus the king who reigned from India even unto Ethiopia. The king sat on his throne in the third of year of his reign, when he made a feast unto his princes and his servants, the power of Persia and Media, the nobles and princes of the 127 provinces which he ruled. Also, Vashti the first lady, the queen, made a feast for the women in the royal house which belonged to King Ahasuerus. On the seventh day when the heart of the king was merry with wine that he commanded the seven men in his cabinet to bring Vashti the queen to shew her beauty, but the queen refused to come at the king's commandment. The king sought advice from the men of his inner-circle. One of the men named

Memucan gave advise that the queen should be put away for her refusal to come and show her beauty, saying this deed by the queen will cause women to despise their husbands. With this the queen was put away, but then the king missed his wife, so he was advised to get a new wife.

2. Esther the chosen queen: Chapter 2: 1-9 Mordecai's uncle's daughter, who lived with him and had a simple lifestyle, was brought to the palace with other young women, when one would be chosen to take the place of Vashti. Esther was chosen because of her simple lifestyle and so became queen instead of Vashti. However, Esther did not shew her people, the Jews, nor her kindred, for Mordecai her coach had charged her that she should not shew it. As Mordecai was sitting at the gate, he learned that two of the king's chamberlains, Bigthan and Teresh, were wroth or upset and sought to lay hands on the king, or maybe made plans to assassinate the king. Mordecai having learned of their plot, passed on the information to Queen Esther, and after investigation was made, the two men were hanged.

After the two men were hanged, the king promoted Haman the Agagite and advanced him and set his seat above all the princes that were with him. Haman became a big man in the office that the king servants would reverenced him, which he enjoyed, but Mordecai a Jew would not bow nor do him reverence, Haman who loved reverence thought to lay hands on Mordecai for that, but because he learned of Mordecai's people the Jews he thought of killing all of them. Haman said unto the king, there is a certain people scattered abroad and dispersed among the people in all the provinces of thy kingdom. If it be please the king, let it be written that they may be destroyed; and I will pay ten thousands talents of silver to the hands of those that have the have the charge of this business to bring it into the king's treasuries. (That is the best thing Haman felt he can do with his money). Jeremiah 17:9 says, the heart is deceitful above all things, and desperately wicked; who can know it?

The king took his ring from his hand, and gave it unto Haman the

Agagite, the Jews' enemy and gave him liberty to execute his plans, and also use his ring, an authority that only the king should have. The Post or the executive order went out to the 127 of the kings' provinces, to destroy, to kill and to cause to perish all Jews both young and old. The post or decree which cannot be changed according to the laws of the Medes and Persians went out being hastened by the king's commandment.

When Mordecai perceived all that was done, he rent his clothes, put on sackcloth with ashes, and cried with a loud and a bitter cry. Also in every province there were great mourning among the Jews. When Esther got the news, she also was grieved, for Mordecai had sent and commanded Esther saying, think not with thyself that thou shall escape in the king's house, more than all the Jews. Esther then sent a message to Mordecai saying; Go gather together all the Jews that are present in Shushan, and fast for me, I also and my maidens will fast likewise, and so will I go in unto the king which is not according to the law. And if I perish, I perish.

Esther the courageous queen. Now it came to pass on the third day that Esther put on her royal apparel and stood in the inner court of the king's house. And it was so, when the king saw Esther the queen standing in the court, that she obtained favor in his sight: and the king held out to Esther the golden scepter that was in his hand, So Esther drew near and touch the top of the scepter. She was accepted, for no one could come to the king uninvited. The king then ask Esther what is her request. Esther said to the king; if it seem good unto the king, let the king and Haman come this day unto the banquet that I have prepared for him; the queen seeking an opportunity to present the case of the Jews with Haman being present. Haman having received this invitation to attend a banquet with the king and queen, went home joyfully, called his friends and his wife and boasted to them of the glory of his riches, not knowing what experiences he would have. Haman said moreover; Yea Esther the queen did let no man come with the king unto the banquet, yet all this availeth me nothing so long as I see Mordecai. Then said Zeresh his wife and all his friends unto him.

Let a gallows be made of fifty cubits high, and tomorrow speak thou unto the king that Mordecai may be hanged thereon; then go thou in merrily with the king unto the banquet. And the thing pleased Haman, and he caused the gallows to be made.

Mordecai exalted: On the night that Haman made the gallows to hang Mordecai; On that night, the king could not sleep, and he commanded to bring the book of records of the chronicles, and they were read before the king, and there it was found written, that Mordecai had told of Bigthana and Teresh, sought to lay hand on the king Ahasuerus. And the king said. What honor and dignity hath been done to Mordecai for this, the king servants said, There is nothing done for him. Now Haman had come to speak unto the king to hang Mordecai on the gallows that he had prepared for him. Haman came in, and the king said unto him. What shall be done unto the man whom the king delighteth to honor?

Haman thought in his heart. To whom would the king delight to do honor more than myself, so he said; Let the royal apparel be brought which the king useth to wear, and the horse that the king rideth upon, and the crown royal which is set upon his head. And let this apparel and horse be delivered to the hand of one of the kings most noble princes, that they array the man withal whom the king delighteth to honor, and bring him on horseback through the streets of the city and proclaim before him. Thus shall it be done to the man whom the king delighteth to honor. Then the king said to Haman, Make haste, and take the apparel and the horse, as thou hast said, and do even so to Mordecai the Jew.

Haman hanged. The king and Haman came to the banquet with Esther the queen, and there Esther presented her case on Haman's intention, and the gallows he prepared to hang Mordecai upon. The king said hang him (Haman) thereon, so they hang Haman on the gallows he had prepared for Mordecai. Then Queen Esther made petition for the reversal of the decree to kill all the Jews, which was granted. So instead of the 13th day of the 12th month be a day of mourning and death, it turns out to be a day of feasting and gladness, and the day of feasting is called the feast of Purim unto this day by the Jews. The first decree went out being hasten by the king's command. The second decree went out being hasten and pressed by the king's command. This speaks of God who is slow to anger but plenteous in mercy.

Notes:

97 – Women in the Bible Who God Used to Accomplish His Purposes

The Woman of Samaria—John 4:1–41

It has been said that nothing happens by accident because God knows all things. The woman spoken of in the passage was in the right place at the right time. That there be a turning point in her life, and in the lives of many in the city of Samaria, God moved in her heart to go and draw water at the time she did. With this we see:

1. The meeting with the Savior John 4 vs. 6–7. The circumstances which brought about that meeting were: Now Jacob's well was there, Jesus being wearied with his journey, sat by the well, and it was the sixth hour. Then cometh a woman of Samaria to draw water; Jesus opened a conversation with the words "Give me to drink," the woman said, thou being a Jew, askest drink of me, which am a woman of Samaria? For the Jews have no dealings with the Samaritans.

2. The message of the Savior John 4 vs. 13–14. Jesus answered and said unto her; Whosoever drinketh of this water shall thirst again; but whosoever drinketh of the water that I shall give him shall never thirst, but the water that I shall give him shall be in him a well of water springing up into everlasting life. Response, the woman said, vs 15 give me this water.

3. The mission for the Savior John 4 vs. 28–29. The woman then left her water-pot and went her way into the city, and said to the men; Come, see a man which told me all things that ever I did: is not this the Christ? She was so excited that she left her water-pot and went to the city to tell others. When a person receives Christ as Savior, there is an amazing joy and satisfaction that drives him to tell others about Christ.

4. The movement of the people John 4 vs. 30–41. Then they went out of the city and came unto him. And many of the Samaritans of that city believed on him for the saying of the woman, which testified, He told me all that ever I did. So when the Samaritans were come to him, they besought him that he would tarry with them: and he abode there two days. And many more believed because of his own word;

We have not been told how many came to Jesus and how many believed in him, but this we see in this story: one woman met Christ, one woman accepted him as the Christ, and one woman witnessed for him. Many believed on him. There is no gender as to whom God will use to spread his word. He will use anyone who surrenders to Him.

Notes:

98 – Youth for Christ and Adults Also

2 Chronicles 34:1–7

*H*ow old should one be to know and serve the Lord, and what background should one have before he should know and serve the Lord? Is it imperative that he should come from a religious family? Should he have had Sunday school training or should he be born on the mission field and have gone to church all the time? Let's look at a few young persons who made their own decision to put their trust in the Lord and came to be examples for many young people and adults also.

1. **Josiah, the young king seeking after God—2 Chronicles 34:1–17.**
    The background of Josiah. Josiah was the great grandson of King Hezekiah, a good king 2 Chr. 29–32. He was the grandson of King Manasseh, a wicked king but repented in times of affliction 2 Chr. 33. He was the son of King Amon, a wicked king that only lasted two years in his reign 2 Chr. 33:21–24. So Josiah did not have a father as a role model, but he sought the Lord in the eight years of his reign. He was then sixteen years old 2 Chr. 34:1–2. With this we see means *salvation.*

    Josiah the young king, in the 12th year of his reign, purged Judah and Jerusalem from evil worship vs. 3b–7 when he was twenty years old. We see *separation.* There is a chorus which says:

    > *Things are different now, something happened to me;*
    > *When I gave my heart to Jesus.*
    > *Things are different now, what change has been made;*
    > *Since I gave my heart to him.*
    > *Things I loved before have gone away;*
    > *Things I love far more have come to stay;*
    > *Things are different now something happened to me;*

When I gave my heart to Him.

Josiah the young king repaired the house of the Lord vs. 8–13. In the 18th year of his reign, he repaired the house of the Lord when he was twenty-four years old. With this we see *service*.

Josiah the young king while engaged in service found the book of the Law of Moses from the workers repairing the house of God vs. 14–17. With this we see *revelation*.

Application: when we believe on the Lord Jesus Christ, that is salvation.

When we are changed in our attitudes and behavior, that we hate sin, that is *separation*.

When we are then engaged in serving the Lord in what and wherever God directs us, that is service. And in doing the Lord's work and studying the Bible, God reveals many of the truths to us, and we grow in grace. That is *revelation*.

2. **Jabez, A young man praying unto God 1 Chr. 4:9–10.** Oh that Thou wouldest bless me indeed, and enlarge my coast, and that thine hand might be with me, and that thou wouldest keep me from evil, that it may not grieve me! And God granted him that which he requested. We see the request of Jabez, the reliance of Jabez, and the reward to Jabez. God granted unto him that which he requested.

3. **A young maid witnessing for God 2 Kings 5:1–14.** Her name is not given because it is not necessary for the story. Naaman captain of the host of the king of Syria, was a great man with his master, and honorable, because by him the Lord had given deliverance unto Syria, he was also a mighty man in valour, but he was a leper. And the Syrians had gone out by companies, and had brought away captives, or POWs, out of the land of Israel a little maid, and she waited on Naaman's wife.

This little maid knew that God uses prophets to do miracles, including healing of people, so when she saw Naaman in his condition, she said to her mistress, Would God my lord were with the prophet that is in Samaria! For he would recover him of his leprosy The young maid had knowledge as to where help could be found. The young maid witnessed for God for the healing of Naaman. He went and was healed of his leprosy.

4. **A young man going away from God Judges 17:6–17.** The young man was from the priestly line, a Levite. He was from the place of worship—Bethlehem-Judah. He was now going where he could find a place, he had no plans or objectives, and for a young man traveling today, I doubt he had a backpack. He was wandering as a homeless stranger. When one do not know the Lord as his savior and has no plans, sometimes that one ends up in the wrong place and with the wrong company. This young man in the book of Judges ended up in the house of Micah, a man who had a house full of gods. This young man got a job there as his priest; he got food and clothing and was content to dwell with Micah. Micah said, Now I know that the Lord will do me good seeing I have a Levite to be my priest. In other words, Now I have a real priest.

Application: many a young person makes a serious mistake and is led away in the wrong direction, but this applies to all ages, so we must be careful.

Trust in the Lord with all thine heart, and lean not unto thine own understanding; In all thy ways acknowledge him, and he shall direct thy paths Proverbs 3:5 and 6.

Notes:

99 – Zacchaeus, the Short man Whose Desire Was Met
Luke 19: 1-10

Jesus, on His way to Jerusalem, passed through Jericho. There was a man named Zacchaeus who was chief among the publicans, and he was rich. He heard that Jesus was passing by. Though he had all that he needed for his physical needs, there was something he wanted that would bring full satisfaction to his life. He wanted to see Jesus, but he had one limitation: he was too short for the crowd then present, but would that stop him from his desires? He would not be stopped by the circumstances, so he ran before the crowd and climbed upon a sycamore tree to see Jesus, for he was to pass that way. There are times when people are deprived from seeing some great person on a parade route because they are too short. But Zacchaeus came up with a plan, and his desire was met.

Zacchaeus climbed a tree so that he would not miss the opportunity, and Jesus was not passing that way again. Zacchaeus did not know that Jesus would see him, but as Jesus pass that way he looked up and saw him. Jesus said Zacchaeus make haste and come down, for today I must abide at thy house. Zacchaeus made haste, came down, and received him joyfully. Jesus said unto him This day is salvation come to this house, for so much as he also is a son of Abraham, he is a man of faith. Jesus said, For the son of man is come to seek and to save that which was lost.

Application: Today Jesus is passing by and will come in our house or into our hearts, but we must seek him. His word is, him that cometh unto me I will in no wise cast out John 6:37; Luke 19:10 For the Son of man is come to seek and to save that which was lost. Behold now is the accepted time, behold now is the day of salvation 2 Corinthians 6:2. The songwriter said:

> *A certain man of whom we read,*
> *who lived in days of old,*

Though he was rich he felt his need;
Of something more than then gold.

Chorus
Oh, yes, my friend, there's something more,
something more than gold,
To know your sins are all forgiven,
is something more than gold.

Redemption Song Book, Chorus Section #1
Harper Collins Publishers
77-85 Fulham Palace Road, London, W6-8JB.

Notes:

100 – What We Believe

We believe the Bible containing sixty-six books to be the inspired, infallible word of God, and as such is our final authority in matters of faith and practice to the praise and glory to God 2Timothy 3:16.

We believe in one God revealed to man as Father, Son, and Holy Spirit, co-eternal, co-existent, and co-equal.

We believe the Lord Jesus Christ, the second Person of the Godhead, became flesh, died for our sins, was buried, and the third day rose from the dead. We believe that this same Jesus who died for our sins now appears in the presence of God for us Heb. 9:24.

We believe the Holy Spirit who is the third Person of the Godhead convicts of sin, indwells the believer, and gives enablement to glorify God in matters of faith and practice.

We believe that salvation is obtained only by repentance toward God, and faith in the death, burial, and resurrection of Christ.

We believe in baptism by immersion as a necessary testimony of obedience by the child of God, according to instruction from our Lord Jesus Christ and practiced at the beginning of the church age Act. 2:41.

We believe in the soon coming again of Christ who will take with Him all who believe in Him and have accepted him as Savior.

We believe in the eternal security of the child of God John 3:16; 5:24, and we also believe in the eternal punishment in hell of all who reject Christ as savior.

Notes:

Other books by evangelist Joseph Jeremiah on Amazon.com and Kindle Books (KDP) and Barns & Noble are as follows:

Your Life Now and Beyond, both paperback and hard cover
The Autobiography of Evangelist Joseph Jeremiah, paperback

If this and the other books are a blessing to you, the author would appreciate hearing from you by e-mail or you can write a review. Here is the e-mail address: jere8301@Gmail.com.

The Lord bless thee, and keep thee:
The Lord make his face shine upon thee,
and be gracious unto thee;
The Lord lift up his countenance upon thee,
and give thee peace. (Numbers 6:24–26)

Printed in the United States
By Bookmasters